COURAGEOUS CITIZENS

COURAGEOUS CITIZENS

HOW CULTURE CONTRIBUTES TO SOCIAL CHANGE

European Cultural Foundation
Valiz, Amsterdam

With contributions by
JOHN AKOMFRAH
BORDERLAND FOUNDATION
ROSI BRAIDOTTI
VASYL CHEREPANYN
BOJANA CVEJIĆ
FATIMA EL-TAYEB
FORENSIC ARCHITECTURE
PASCAL GIELEN
STUART HALL
DAVID HARVEY
STEFAN KAEGI
IVAN KRASTEV
WIETSKE MAAS
MARINA NAPRUSHKINA
LIA PERJOVSCHI
SASKIA SASSEN
ANA VUJANOVIĆ
KATHERINE WATSON

COURAGEOUS CITIZENS

FOREWORD
Ivan Krastev

Courage has long been out of fashion in Europe. The revolutions of 1989, for example, were inspiring yet utterly unheroic: the fall of the Soviet-Union brought the battle of political ideals to an abrupt end, with democracy and representative governments, individual and minority rights protection, and prosperity based on open markets winning the hearts and minds for lack of plausible alternatives. Reforms were often treated in the sense of bureaucratic obligations, rather than as a real chances for transformation. Less fortunate parts of the world—where neither welfare nor democracy is on the menu now or in the foreseeable future—also rarely saw (and are unlikely to see) heroic revolutions, as exit. Emigrating to other parts of the world seems the rational choice for many.

Courage is back today as the cardinal civic virtue. What has changed?

The results of the hard institutional work did not meet the high expectations. Both in 'new' Europe, where people almost religiously believed in the promised land of a radiant liberal democratic future, and in 'older' Europe many failed to see the benefits of opening towards the East, deepening EU integration, globalization. The reason was that the benefits were not justly distributed, and the weakest often bore a disproportionate share of the burden. The anxieties of the global crises after 2008 deepened the sense of injustice among those left behind. The 'moral' panic around the refugee crisis fuelled further dissatisfaction with the rapid changes, as many who feared they wouldn't be able to cope saw those changes as a threat. New (or just 'refurbished') leaders seized the moment and started using each opportunity to deepen the ruptures within and between societies rather than offer workable solutions to existing problems. Citizens—in some countries more than in others—often turned into angry majorities, quick to find culprits, be it the cosmopolitan elites, the unpopular minorities, or the universal enemy: the refugees. Rather than healing injustices in their societies, anger and hate deepened them. Dehumanizing the 'enemies' blunted the moral sensitivity to the pain of the different other.

This adverse societal 'climate change' opened a space for the re-emergence of a forgotten figure—that of the courageous citizen. Yet their courage, their revolutionary stance, is different today. They are concerned with our divided societies. Their cause is to rebuild bridges that where broken and to think things through in more inclusive ways. They fight injustice and prejudices, not in battles turned into zero-sum lethal games by fuelled passion, but in conversations and encounters that aim to recover the lost common ground, the lost shared values. Recovering the common ground may allow for fruitful redefinition and questioning of those of our values that are at the root of the injustices and ruptures in our societies. Because deeply beneath a passionate concern for ourselves at the expense of the others, a concern that divides us internally and closes us from without, there may lay hidden a common core—a concern for the joys and the pains of the others, a concern that brought people to live together in a community in the first place.

Culture is the 'natural' space for such reinvented conversation. It keeps the memory of our shared values alive, turning them into moral sensibilities we rarely notice. Contemporary cultural practitioners and social and political activists embody this new meaning of courage—in questioning the status quo, in reinventing the lost meaning of solidarity, they contribute to change and healing in our societies.

Ivan Krastev is the Chairman of the Centre for Liberal Strategies in Sofia and permanent fellow at the Institute for Human Sciences, Vienna.

COURAGEOUS CITIZENS

INTRODUCTION
Bas Lafleur, Wietske Maas and Susanne Mors

Over the past decades, the cultural and political map of Europe has changed rapidly: such developments as the enlargement of the European Union, migration to and within Europe, and the wider repercussions of globalization have posed numerous social and political challenges. Instead of recognizing and valuing these challenges, there has been a growing tendency to retreat into fixed ideas of culture and cultural divides. Since Europe has always been constituted by diversity, the pressing issue has been and still is how people of different languages, memories, representations, and beliefs can live and move together within Europe's changing landscape.

This book advocates the capacity of culture for contributing to social change. It is also a source of inspiration for renegotiating our understanding of the world and affirming culture as a critical space to practice courage and perseverance amid complex societal reconfigurations. Our focus is on courageous citizens: those whose daring, sharing, and inventing contribute to our collective future, and for whom culture and democracy are the starting points for vision and action. Their social energy gives rise to alternative stories, they embrace the underrepresented while opening up space for learning, living together, and questioning the character of democracy, one that is continuously rethought along the way.

Courageous Citizens is published on the occasion of the tenth anniversary of the European Cultural Foundation's Princess Margriet Award for Culture, an annual award acknowledging and amplifying the work of individuals and collectives whose creative work can truly make a difference in Europe's societies.

In this publication, we explore intellectual and practical interventions that open up a terrain of debate in the enduring struggle for just societies across Europe, zooming in on a couple of key themes that have proven to be of particular relevance over the past ten years, and that also keep resonating when looking at the very possibility of better future: (1) Diversity and Equality; (2) Communities and Democracy; and (3) Fragmentation and Solidarity.

We do so by presenting a collection of previously published as well as newly commissioned texts, conversations, and visual work. In all contributions we see an attempt to transform the way we view the world, and concurrently, the potential of culture to contribute to positive social change.

Part I — Diversity and Equality:
Articulating the Political in Culture

Addressing the challenges of *diversity and equality* remains, unfortunately, an urgency. The workings of a desocialized economic paradigm have resulted in extreme inequalities, and confront us with a Europe marked by polarized outlooks on life, values, or beliefs that fuel isolation and radicalization of its inhabitants.

Actively striving to enact diversity and equality across institutions and societies throughout Europe is a significant means to make democracy inclusive to everyone; in this process, culture's faculty to imagine—and enact—the world differently plays a pivotal role in reconfiguring the social fabric, but also serves as a means to achieve a richer intellectual, emotional, ethical, and spiritual existence.

In this part of the book we look at how the principle of inclusivity cannot even be contemplated without equal opportunity and a political say for those excluded from the circles of power through race, gender, and class. Informed by the influential intellectual work of the late Stuart Hall, this section traces the changing discourse and (political) imaginaries on diversity and equality, and how this has been addressed by several thinkers and practitioners in Europe over the last decade.

In 2008, Hall received the ECF Princes Margriet Award for Culture for his exceptional lifework on the practice and ideas of cultural diversity and on bringing about a constructive understanding of what diversity is and may become in society today. He has actively engaged with the political debate, especially with regard to issues of culture and identity. Here we couple his Laudation Speech on 'Cultural Diversity' (2008) —in which Hall stresses the value of institution-building in support of sustainable change—with 'Minimal Selves' (1987), which examines the impossibility of a fully resolved identity from a migrant's perspective.

Relating to that, we asked philosopher Rosi Braidotti to reflect further on the question of Europe today as a site of possible resistance against nationalism and the political economy of our time. We were interested in her take on 'politics of location' and the question of how European identity is constructed and with whom. In her essay, 'Becoming-World: A New Perspective on European Citizenship', Braidotti argues that it is time to re-invent cosmopolitan citizenship in a manner that moves beyond both an a-historical Eurocentrism and a flat repetition of universalism. In order to construct this new kind of cosmopolitan relation, according to Braidotti, the feminist method of politics of location as well as situated knowledge provide the analytical tools to explore our respective locations—including class, gender, ethnicity, et cetera—and confront our differences critically. And, as creative tools they facilitate the mediation of tensions and conflicts and thus support the construction of sharable discourses and practices. This offers an alternative to a sacralized notion of nationalism and allows to shift the question of European citizenship to a matter of shared values and active participation, while dislodging a Eurocentric or any other kind of essentialized identity. In courageously embracing complexity, accountability, and solidarity with both human and non-human 'others', new kinds of transformative European citizenship can be developed in which 'we'—although not one and the same—will be able to 'become-world' together. This image of Europe provides horizons of hope and the possibility of a future that is alive to the positivity of difference and the wealth of diversity.

Widely known in Britain and the larger Anglo-Saxon world, where Stuart Hall's work on culture has actually shaped the very discourse of cultural diversity, we were interested to see if and how cultural studies tools have informed the discussion in other parts of Europe. This was the starting point for our conversation 'Art, Knowledge, and Politics' with Vasyl Cherepanyn, Director of the Visual Culture Research Centre (VCRC) in Kiev, Ukraine. With him we talked about topics such as politicized culture and political subjectivity; identity and citizenship; learning and knowledge *with* and through visual culture. The centre was founded in 2008 as a platform for collaboration among academics, artists, and activists, initially emerging from the Department of Cultural Studies at the National University of Kyiv-Mohyla Academy. In this time of political turmoil in Ukraine, VCRC provides a much-needed meeting ground for social activism and progressive artistic and discursive programming that is making a remarkable contribution to sustaining cultural and political debate across Ukraine and the region.

Among other things, Cherepanyn regretfully addresses what he calls a war on truth and remembering. In response to this, and approaching the end of Part I, we chose to feature images from Forensic Architecture's investigative project *77sqm_9:26min.* For this project, the German citizens' and activist alliance 'Unravelling the NSU Complex', together with Haus der Kulturen der Welt Berlin and documenta 14, had commissioned Forensic Architecture to investigate unresolved aspects of one of the crimes committed by a neo-Nazi group between 2000 and 2007. In addition to a written report, this resulted in a three-channel video presenting the results of the research, which was present-ed for the first time during documenta 14 in Kassel. Following the Latin etymology of 'forensis', which pertains to the forum, Forensic Architecture examines and assembles various testimo-nies with the help of ground-breaking technological, architectural, and aesthetic methods to tell and visualize an intricate and inclusive story. Today, they provide crucial evidence for interna-tional courts and work with activist groups, NGO's, Amnesty International, and the UN. Their work shows how architecture as a field of knowledge and cultural practice can play an active role in struggles for justice.

Part II — Communities and Democracy:
Emerging Alternatives

In recent years, we have seen a growing gap between people and the institutions that democratically represent them. The rapidly shrinking belief in a unified Europe and the increasing distrust of 'Brussels' (resulting in, for example, Brexit and the rise of 'populist' Euro-scepticism across EU member states) are compelling exam-ples of this. Exclusionary practices, be it economically, politically, or culturally motivated, have created deep divides in and between communities across Europe. At the same time, citizens themselves are exploring new collaborative approaches to decision-making, activism, and engaged citizenship, often on a local level yet resonating on a wider scale. Powerful bottom-up social movements have emerged, developing new participatory democratic practices that challenge existing structures and contribute to social change. This section focuses on the important role of citizens' movements in changing the political and economic status quo. We start off with a conversation with renowned urban geogra-pher David Harvey, titled 'Culture, Commons, and the Right to the City'. Initially held in 2013 during the 'Citizenship, Orientalism and Commons' conference, Harvey first spoke about the need for traditions of commoning to grow and insisted that neither the state nor private interests should stop citizens from exercising right in their city. Now we asked him to revisit these topics and to answer a couple of additional questions that came to mind when comparing the situation in 2013 with that of today. Our questions focused on the role of citizen engagement in increasing social justice, how the idea of people as citizens is currently endangered by the increasing emphasis on entrepreneurial subjectivity, and where Harvey sees possibilities for citizenship in countries that are progressively turning into authoritarian regimes—where what is 'regular' citizenship in one context becomes 'courageous' citizenship in another. As a strong proponent of the notion of the right to the city, David Harvey emphasizes its importance in the struggle against current political-economic systems that reinforce the development of authoritarian politics.

The idea of the right of the city is the starting point of sociologist Pascal Gielen's contribution to the present volume, 'The Global Civil Parade: Constitutions of Transnational Citizenship'. He argues that the past decade has seen a shift in the understanding of the notion of citizenship, from a *formal* one that concerns the legal status of a citizen to a *moral* normative interpretation of what a *good* citizen should be or do. This shift towards a moral discourse is also seen in the political arena, where the idea that the nature of democracy should continuously be the topic of discussion now commonly seems to have been replaced by the rhetoric of active citizenship and participative society. With this moralistic rhetoric the right to citizenship does not seem to be open to anyone anymore. At first sight this seems to be rather negative, but Gielen points out a remarkable positive effect of this shift, in the emergence of numerous citizens' initiatives and social movements such as Occupy throughout the world, which are indicative of a new vitality in the civil sphere around the globe. In this 'global civil parade' Gielen not only sees the first outlines of an emerging transnational citizenship, but also the signs of a new democracy in the making, that may prove to become a viable replacement for our current neoliberal representative democracies.

While these activist and citizens' initiatives seem to be part of a global phenomenon, Pascal Gielen points out that in many cases they only operate on a local level. A similar point is made by Bojana Cvejić and Ana Vujanović, both active in the field of contemporary performing arts, in their essay 'The Crisis of the Social Imaginary and Beyond', where they consider these initiatives and movements until now to have largely been the preserve of a relatively small group of citizens. What they perceive in society today is a general crisis of social imagination, which manifests itself not only in politics but also in the fields of culture and the arts. Taking the contemporary performance arts scenes in Europe as an example, they do see sharp critiques on individualistic and collective capitalism, but not an affirmation of any possible alternatives, only provisional proposals. At the same time, they do consider art a possible space for imagining the social. Having outlined the negative aspects of the crisis of the social imagination, they affirm the elements and traces of emergent social imaginaries that are being developed on a larger scale in Europe and beyond.

Picking up on the notion of individual considerations and how they bump up against societal ones, we close this part with works by artist and activist Lia Perjovschi. She has been recognized as one of the leading performance artists in Romania, but is perhaps best known for her Contemporary Art Archive/ Center for Art Analysis and for the diagrammatic Timelines and Mind Maps that she has been drawing since the 1990s. With these drawings, which consist entirely of handwritten words, Perjovschi traces networks of interrelations and convergences that she has uncovered between different concepts. These diagrams are part of what she has called a Contemporary Art Archive (CAA) Kit, in which they function as recuperative tools that contribute to the creation of both local and transnational communities. In three selected diagrams, one of which was specifically drawn for this publication, she explores 'how to change the world as an individual', associates on the notions of courageous citizens in relation to social change, and looks into a possible—though not always inevitable or bright—future.

Part III — Fragmentation and Solidarity:
Making New Connections

The first decades of the twenty-first century have witnessed a fragmented and polarized world that has had an increasingly divisive effect on European citizens. Moreover, in a number of European countries (whether or not members of the EU), ris ng authoritarianisms and xenophobic, populist sentiments are becoming more legitimized. In addition, the forced movement of people—either fleeing conflict, or for economic, social, or environmental reasons—has posed an enormous challenge on top of tensions related to social and economic inequality and fear of being left out. However, there are a myriad of artists, creatives, thinkers, collectives, and communities who are standing up and finding ways to think and act through culture to thwart such divisiveness.

In this section of the book we discuss and highlight inspiring examples of fresh thinking and practices that try to connect and integrate what otherwise seems to be falling apart. We start with a text by sociologist Saskia Sassen, who is well known for her studies on cities, immigration, and states in the world economy, with inequality, gendering, and digitization as three key variables running though her work. In her essay, 'The Language of Expulsion', Sassen points out that the language commonly used to describe inequality and social exclusion no longer works. Hence, she argues for radically new ways of addressing deeper trends in society at large that cut across familiar divisions, and which might be easily overlooked in more traditional analyses bound to, for instance, national borders. She focuses on what she calls expulsions—people being expelled from work or their homes through the abuses of democratic systems through powerful corporations: the scale of which has become so extreme, and interconnected on a global scale, that existing conceptual categories can no longer capture it.

From Saskia Sassen's global perspective, we then turn to the European context with cultural historian Fatima El-Tayeb's essay 'European Others', originally written for the European Cultural Foundation/Doc Next Network publication *Remixing Europe* (2014). She looks at the position of racialized communi- t es in the European Union, arguing that the tension between a growing non-white, non-Christian population and essentialist definitions of Europeanness produces new forms of identity and activism. Against the background of the anxiety-ridden debate around perceived threats to a European identity, she looks into the consequences of a long history of racism in Europe on the representation of communities of colour and so-called migrants as the eternal Other. At the same time, El-Tayeb highlights modes of cultural resistance in which exclusionary structures are being questioned throughout Europe, thereby creating a Europeanization movement from below in which migrant and minority communities challenge the ideology of racelessness that expels them from the community of citizens.

From El-Tayeb's reflective stance towards multiple identities—which echoes Stuart Hall's notion of politics of difference—we move to a striking local example of a hands-on community of practice based in Berlin. In her work as an artist, Marina Naprushkina examines the structure of authoritarian systems to determine the role of art and creative activism in changing the political status quo. Since 2013, Naprushkina is one of the forces behind Neue Nachbarschaft//Moabit, a self-organizing community in the Berlin neighbourhood Moabit with self-empowerment at its heart. It is here that old and new Berliners are finding collaborative ways of living together, opening up art's potential to contribute to Europe's common future. We are publishing a selection of columns from her book *Neue Heimat? Wie Flüchtlinge uns zu besseren Nachbarn machen* (*'Neue Heimat'? How Refugees Make Us Better Neighbours*; 2015), in which she dismantles the dire reality of refugees trying to find a new home in German society.

Artist, filmmaker, and cultural activist John Akomfrah's images are a confluence of diasporic memory, a haunting reverberation of stories of migration across time and space. His works are characterized by their investigations into memory, postcolonialism, and temporality, and often explore the experiences of migrant diasporas globally. We are delighted to feature three triptychs made especially for this publication, titled *The Unending Enigmas of Arrival.* The scenes are set among the architectural ruins of a former airport in southern Greece, a space of endlessly deferred departure or arrival.

We end this publication with an epilogue by Katherine Watson, reminding us of the occasion for this book: 10 Years ECF Princess Margriet Award for Culture. It is a moment to take stock and to acknowledge all those courageous people in and across Europe, both visible and invisible, who strive—sometimes risking what they have in doing so—to change existing structures for the better. Katherine Watson's text is followed by images of theatre performances by Borderland Foundation and Stefan Kaegi (Rimini Protokoll), two of the ECF Princess Margriet Award Laureates of the past ten years whose work is intrinsically participative—through always working with and for people who are directly involved in the issues addressed.

COURAGEOUS CITIZENS

The scope of this publication does by no means allow for a complete and exhaustive overview and acknowledgement of all initiatives that fall under the remit of the three chosen themes. Nonetheless we do hope to have given a glimpse of not only the dilemmas and dynamics but also of the potential of culture and critical thinking to substantially contribute to social change in a Europe that is unlearning itself as a centre by listening to the world speak back.

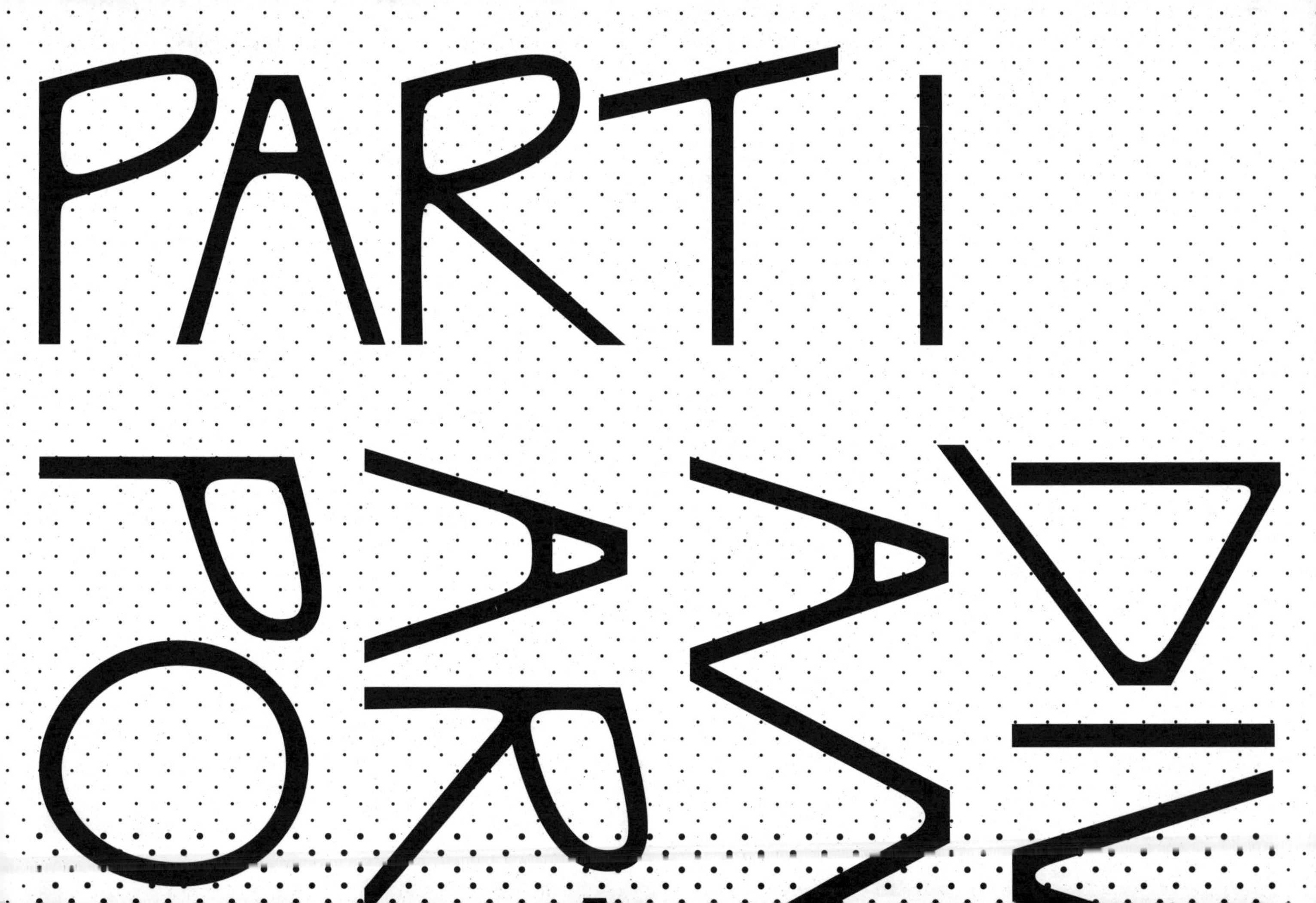
PART I

ERSI T

D EQ O

TIK U

ITIKA V

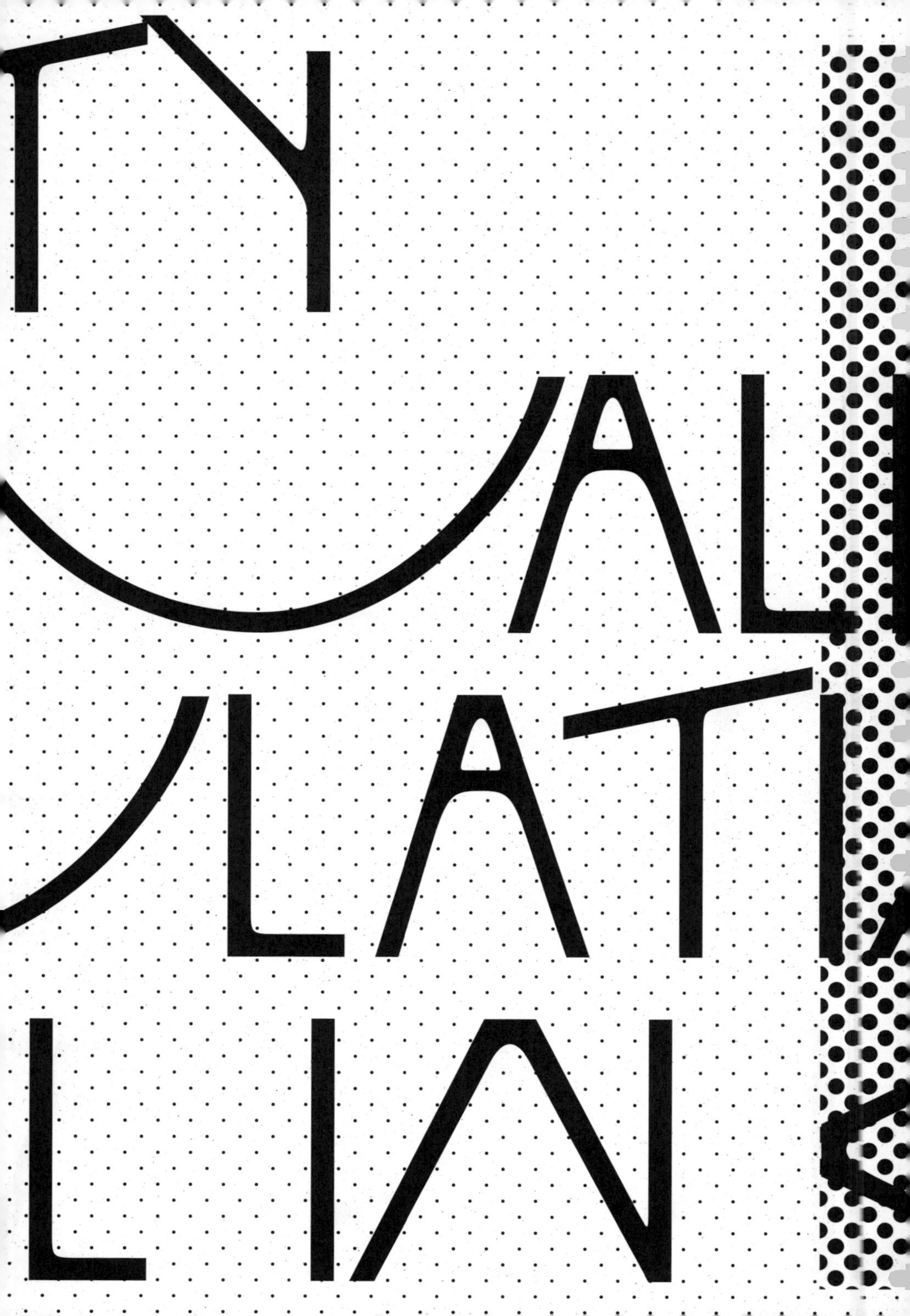

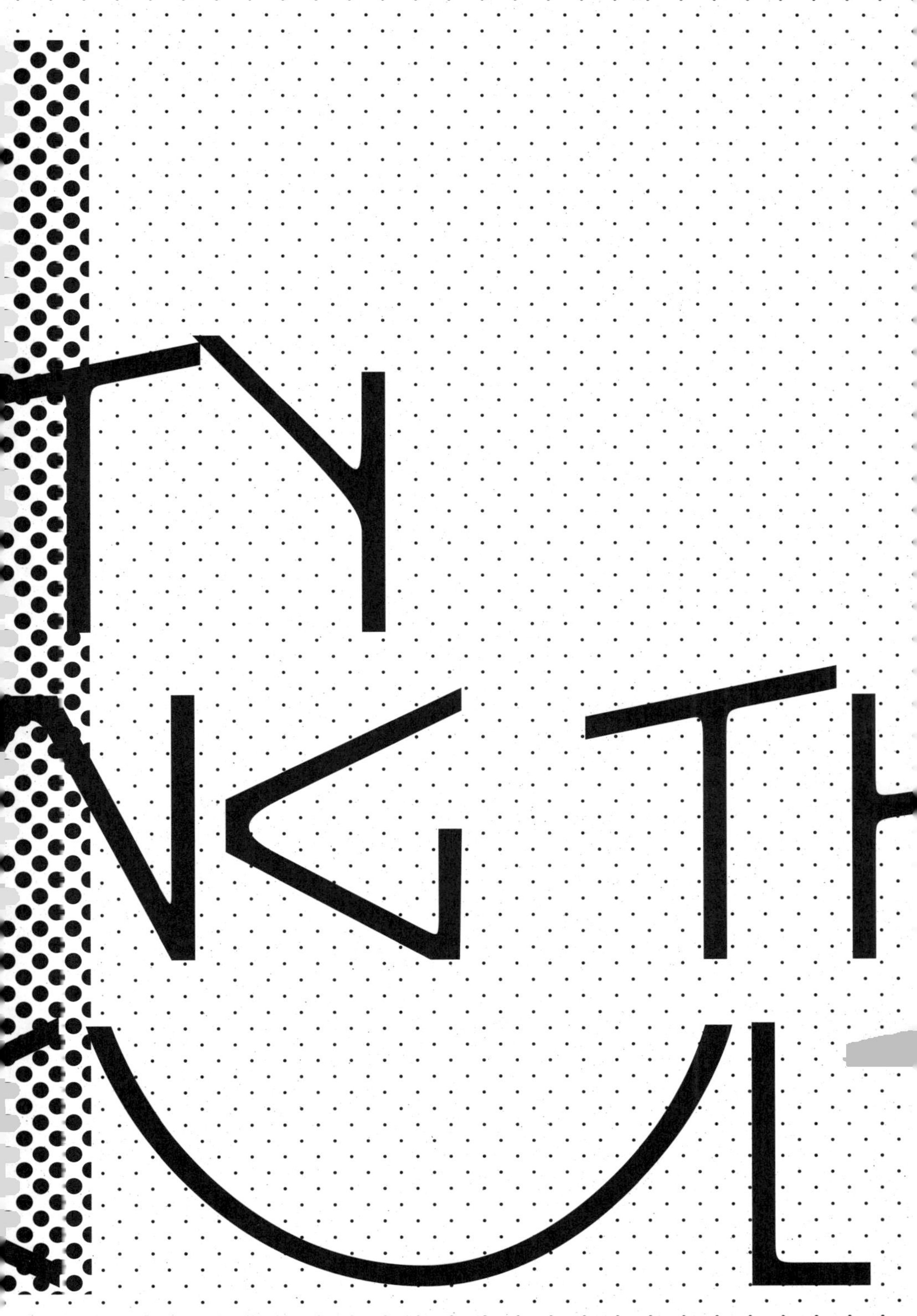

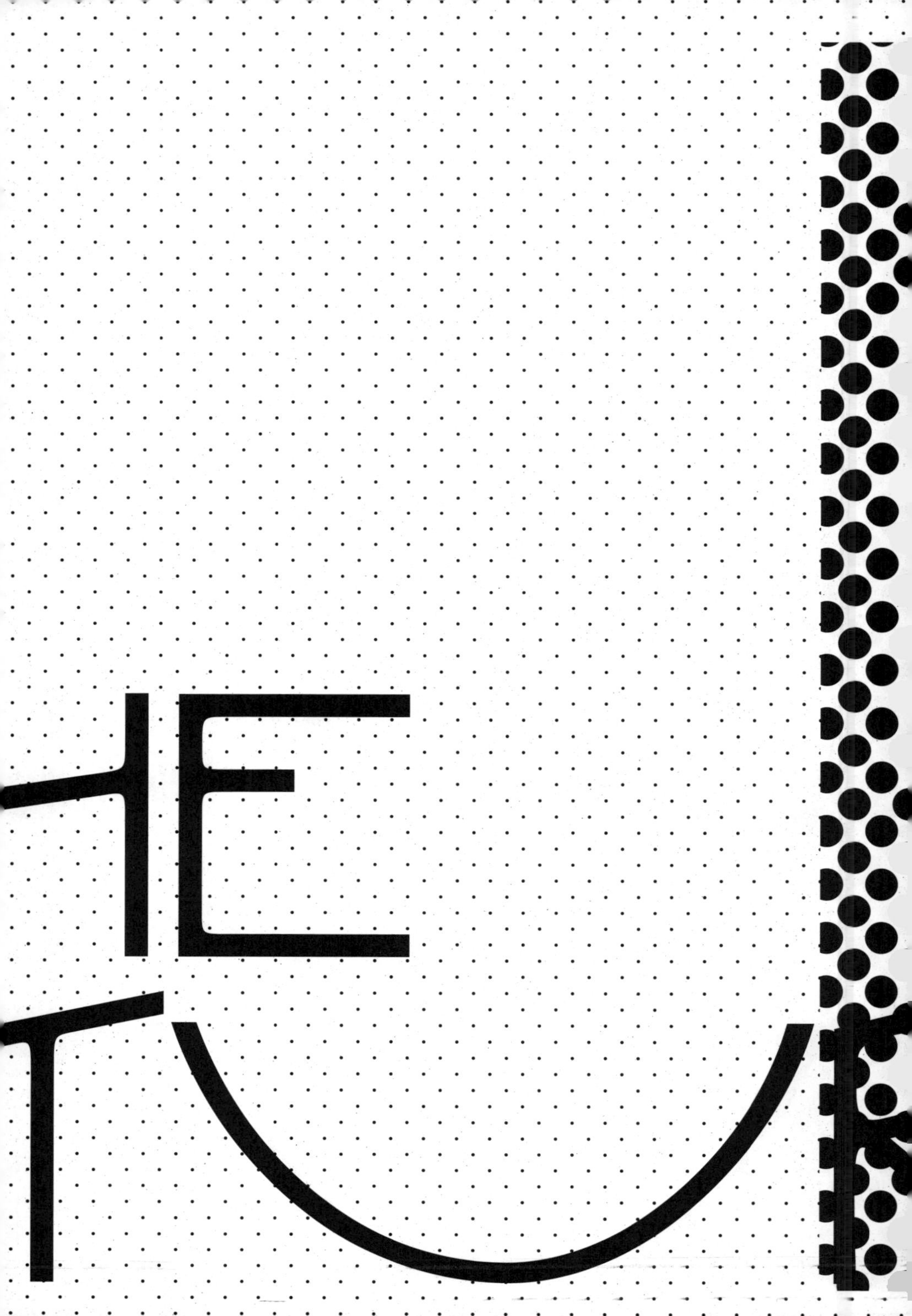

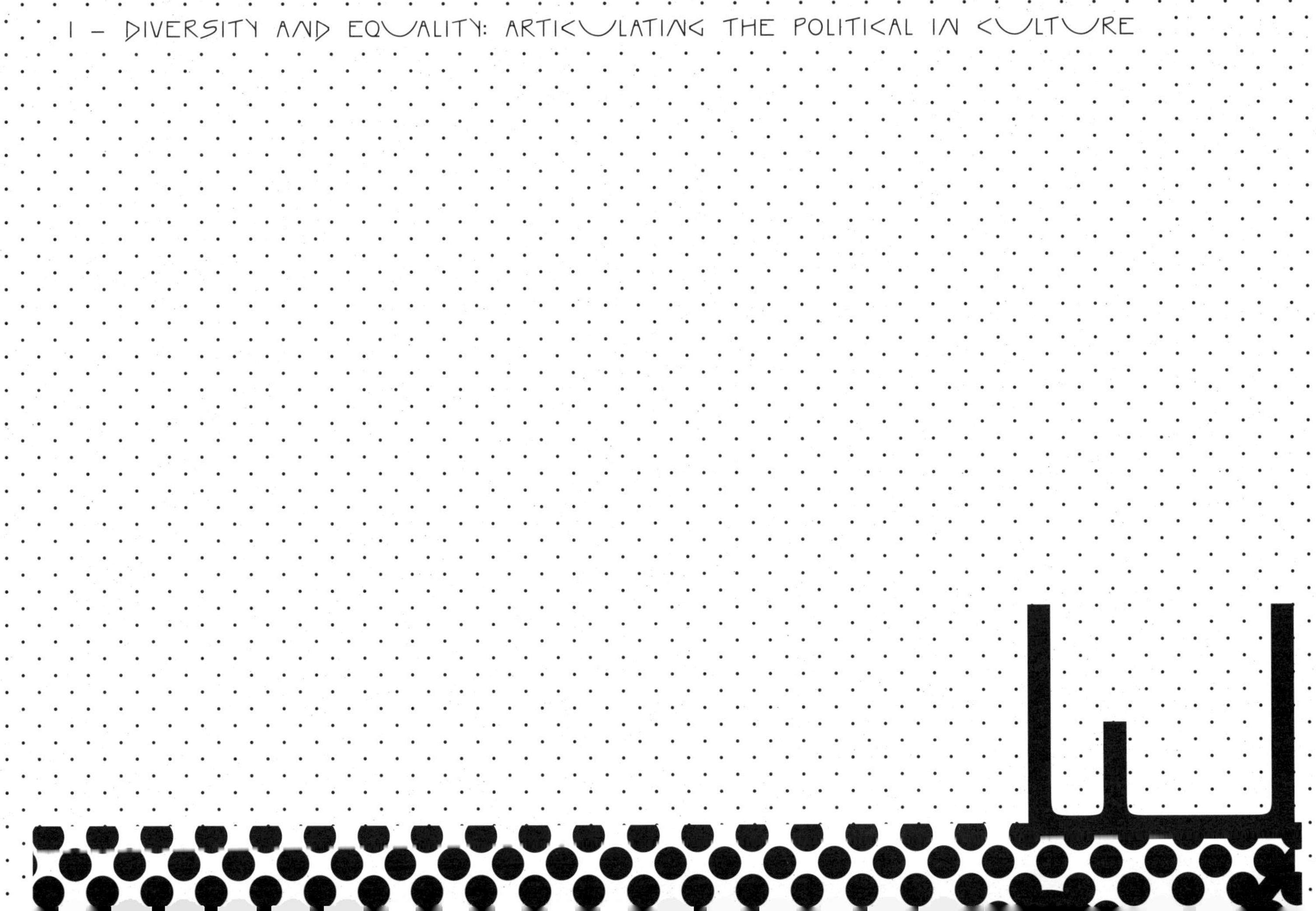

1 – DIVERSITY AND EQUALITY

CULTURAL DIVERSITY

Stuart Hall

1 — DIVERSITY AND EQUALITY

I have been involved with cultural diversity work, one way or another, since I first arrived in Europe from Jamaica in 1951. My arrival was more or less coterminous with the onset of those post-war migrations that initiated the contemporary history of, triggered the debate about the 'cultural diversity' idea. They marked the formation of new diasporas at the heart of European historic towns and cities, posing deep questions about cultural homogeneity and heterogeneity long before the term 'cultural diversity' was first coined. It is worth reminding you that I came to Europe as a colonial subject and, as such, was the product of a much longer 'encounter' between Europe and its 'others' around the world—though 'encounter' may be too euphemistic a way of describing that long and troubled history. The post-war migrations are rightly seen as initiating a new phase in the conversation about the inter-face between cultural traditions.

There is a strongly-held view that the inter-mingling with different cultures will inevitably weaken and ruin our own. We are therefore tempted to represent our own cultures as more homogenous than in fact they are. We often feel impelled to retreat from the difficulties of dialogue by withdrawing, defensively, into the safe fortresses of our own cultures in the face of the challenge of difference. In our post-9/11 world, difference—with its threat of the unknown, the unfamiliar and its danger of separate but parallel worlds—has come to be seen as dangerous and threatening. It has become fashionable in Britain to say that 'multiculturalism is dead'—and that 9/11 et cetera killed it off.

In the face of this, one strategy is to return to our 'roots' which seem to provide the guarantee of our identities back to the mists—if not the myths—of time, and the sources of social cohesion. But one of the difficult truths that migrants learn, and which may carry a metaphorical lesson for us all, is that, in truth, we can't 'go home again'. The past is not waiting for us, back there, unchanged, as a place of comfort and solace. The past is being transformed before our very eyes and some are being deeply unhinged, by the forces of contemporary globalization. It has therefore become imperative to think more about our 'routes', that is to say, the very different pathways which different cultures, peoples, traditions, languages, and religions have taken to the present; which have brought us into, and convened us—some would say *conscripted* us all—to the same spaces and times in an increasingly globalized world.

Cultural difference is not about to disappear. It is not a temporary, little local difficulty which a dollop of goodwill on all sides will dissolve. It is a difficult and a hard taskmaster. This is because it is the product of what we must call the 'combined and uneven character' of globalization, which is a deeply contradictory and unequal process: creating the dim and remote hope of greater universalism and integration on one side, while on the other side its lived realities arise from the paces and stages of development, the deep and apparently ineradicable chasms between rich and poor, the powerful and the powerless, the replete and the hungry, the healthy and the sick, the blessed and the damned of the earth.

The only alternative, the necessary strategy we have, is to recognize and learn to value difference despite its difficulties; to learn through practice, through trial and error, how, slowly and sometimes painfully, to negotiate difference. We need to conduct those life experiments that create the conditions in which difference can 'play' creatively across the traditional cultural categories; how, in short, to live with difference so as to make it into a creative rather than a destructive force. Whatever you think of Salman Rushdie, I think he was correct to say that the intermingling of cultures, the 'transformation that comes from new and unexpected combinations of human beings, cultures, ideas, politics, movies, and songs' is one of the principal ways in which, historically, 'newness enters the world.'

Cultural diversity is the name we give to a certain kind of 'learning', which gives us insight into the inner landscapes of how other people live their lives, how they experience and dream their worlds; how they cope with the broken hopes and possibilities of making a new life in a strange land; how they try to resolve the contradictory realities of belongingness; and how they, in turn—disturbingly—see into ours. It teaches us how to express, to find significant form, whatever the medium, for our innermost thoughts, feelings, and desires. Learning through culture and the arts works by indirection. It is the slow, mutual, dialogic unfolding of reciprocal understanding. It 'teaches' us in ways that pure information, knowledge of the rational and logical kind, cannot supply. It constitutes in practice that acknowledgement of our radical dependence on 'the other'; on 'the other' who completes us, who is our 'constitutive outside'; on what Jacques Lacan called that radically de-centring experience of seeing ourselves 'from the place of the other'. It may stop us from projecting our fears and anxieties—the 'bad' parts of ourselves—into 'the other'. This is a kind of 'knowledge' that teaches us how to listen and look, to learn through listening and looking, and vice versa. It learns through the body, as well as the mind and the intellect. Its terrain is that of the imagination.

This is a matter for cultures and societies as a whole. But cultural institutions have a special role to play in the process. However, they often remain embedded in older institutional cultures, connected to traditional artistic elites and to existing political frameworks; or they have become enmeshed in the 'spectacle' of the festivals and biennales, which represent global difference as a sort of simulacrum, a ventriloquizing of diversity, driven mainly by the global market. Can they really open, or be made to open, themselves to the radical project of learning to live with difference, to the emerging possibilities of a diverse, pluri-centred cultural world? Or are they likely to remain part of the problem rather than part of the solution?

I have spent some time institution-building for cultural diversity. Not because I have any special skill in this area, but because, without institutions, creative efforts, like the rainbow, come and go, often leaving no trace behind them; or alternatively they become monuments to themselves. To repeat a sentiment I recently expressed on the occasion of the opening of Rivington Place, the building dedicated to cultural diversity in the visual arts which we opened last October in Shoreditch, London: 'It's not worth keeping an institution alive for one minute more after it ceases to open a space that makes certain possibilities possible.' Otherwise, institution-building is simply a drag— as well as being a drag on history.

I want to take this opportunity to express my deep gratitude to Her Royal Highness, Princess Margriet, to the European Cultural Foundation, and to the Dutch Ministries of Culture and Foreign Affairs for initiating this award; and for doing me the great honour of making me a joint laureate (with Jérôme Bel and Pichet Klunchun) in its first year. I am particularly pleased to receive the award from Prinses Margriet of the Netherlands who, in her presidency of the Foundation, has done so much to promote the cause of cultural diversity; and I am especially delighted to be one of its recipients in 2008, the European Year of Intercultural Dialogue.

This text is a transcript of the laudation speech that Stuart Hall (1932–2014) gave on 9 December 2008 in Brussels, after having received the 2008 ECF Princess Margriet Award for Culture.

1 – DIVERSITY AND EQUALITY

MINIMAL SELVES

Stuart Hall

1 — DIVERSITY AND EQUALITY

A few adjectival thoughts only...

Thinking about my own sense of identity, I realize that it has always depended on the fact of being a *migrant*, on the *difference* from the rest of you. So one of the fascinating things about this discussion is to find myself centred at last. Now that, in the postmodern age, you all feel so dispersed, I become centred. What I've thought of as dispersed and fragmented comes, paradoxically, to be *the* representative modern experience! This is 'coming home' with a vengeance! Most of it I much enjoy—welcome to migranthood. It also makes me understand something about identity that has been puzzling me in the last three years.

I've been puzzled by the fact that black people in London today are marginalized, fragmented, unenfranchized, disadvantaged, and dispersed. And yet, they look as if they own the territory. Somehow, they too, in spite of everything, are centred, in place: without much material support, it's true, but nevertheless, they occupy a new kind of space at the centre. And I've wondered again and again: what is it about the long discovery-rediscovery of identity among blacks in this migrant situation that allows them to lay a kind of claim to certain parts of the earth which aren't theirs, with quite that certainty? I do feel a sense of—dare I say—envy surrounding them. Envy is a very funny thing for the British to feel at this moment in time—to want to be black! Yet I feel some of you superstitiously moving towards that marginal identity. I welcome you to that, too.

Now the question is: is this centring of marginality really *the* representative postmodern experience? I was given the title 'the minimal self'. I know the discourses that have theoretically produced that concept of 'minimal self'. But my experience now is that what the discourse of the postmodern has produced is not something new but a kind of recognition of where identity always was at. It is in that sense that I want to redefine the general feeling that more and more people seem to have about themselves: that they are all, in some way, *recently migrated*, if I can coin that phrase.

The classic questions that every migrant faces are twofold: 'Why are you here?' and 'When are you going back home?' No migrant ever knows the answer to the second question until asked. Only then does she or he know that really, in the deep sense, she/he's never going back. Migration is a one-way trip. There is no 'home' to go back to. There never was. But 'why are you here' is also a really interesting question, which I've never been able to find a proper answer to either. I know the reasons one is supposed to give: 'for education', 'for the children's sake', 'for a better life, more opportunities', 'to enlarge the mind', et cetera. The truth is, I am here because it's where my family is not. I really came here to get away from my mother. Isn't that the universal story of life? One is where one is to try and get away from somewhere else. That was the story I could never tell anybody about myself. So I had to find other stories, other fictions, which were more authentic or, at any rate, more acceptable, in place of the Big Story, of the endless evasion of patriarchal family life. Who I am—the 'real' me—was formed in relation to a whole set of other narratives. I was aware of the fact that identity is an invention from the very beginning, long before I understood any of this theoretically. Identity is formed at the unstable point where the 'unspeak-able' stories of subjectivity meet the narratives of history, of a culture. And since he/she is positioned in relation to cultured narratives that have been profoundly expropriated, the colonized subject is always 'somewhere else': doubly marginalized, displaced always *other* than where he or she is, or is able to speak from.

It wasn't a joke when I said that I migrated in order to get away from my family. I did. The problem, one discovers, is that since one's family is always already 'in here', there is no way in which you can actually leave them. Of course, sooner or later, they recede in memory, or even in life. But these are not the 'burials' that really matter. I wish they were still around, so that I didn't have to carry them around, locked up somewhere in my head, from which there is no migration. So from the first, in relation to them, and then to all other symbolic 'others', I certainly was always aware of the self as only constituted in that kind of absent-present contestation with something else, with some other 'real me', which is and isn't there.

If you live, as I've lived, in Jamaica, in a lower-middle class family that was trying to be a middle-class Jamaican family trying to be an upper-middle-class Jamaican family trying to be an English Victorian family... I mean the notion of displacement as a place of 'identity' is a concept you learn to live with, long before you are able to spell it. Living with, living through difference. I remember the occasion when I returned to Jamaica on a visit sometime in the early 1960s, after the first wave of migration to England, and my mother said to me: 'Hope they don't think you are one of those immigrants over there!' And of course, at that point I knew for the first time I was an immigrant. Suddenly in relation to that narrative of migration, one version of the 'real me' came into view. I said: 'Of course I'm an immigrant. What do you think I am?' And she said in that classic Jamaican middle-class way, 'Well, I hope the people over there will shove all the immigrants off the long end of a short pier.' (They've been shoving ever since).

The trouble is that the instant one learns to be 'an immigrant', one recognizes one can't be an immigrant any longer: it isn't a tenable place to be. I then went through the long, important, political education of discovering that I am 'black'. Constituting oneself as 'black' is another recognition of self through difference: certain clear polarities and extremities against which one tries to define oneself. We constantly underestimate the importance, to certain crucial political things that have happened in the world, of this ability of people to constitute themselves, psychically, in the black identity. It has long been thought that this is really a simple process: a recognition, a resolution of irresolutions, a coming to rest in some place that was always there waiting for one. The 'real me' at last!

The fact is, 'black' has never been just there either. It has always been an unstable identity, psychically, culturally, and politically. It, too, is a narrative, a story, a history. Something constructed, told, spoken, not simply found. People now speak of the society I come from in totally unrecognizable ways. Of course Jamaica is a black society, they say. In reality it is a society of black and brown people who lived for three or four hundred years without ever being able to speak of themselves as 'black'. Black is an identity that had to be learned and could only be learned in a certain moment. In Jamaica that moment is the 1970s. So the notion that identity is a simple—if I can use the metaphor—black or white question, has never been the experience of black people, at least in the diaspora. These are 'imaginary communities'—and not a bit the less real because they are also symbolic. Where else could the dialogue of identity between subjectivity and culture take place?

I – DIVERSITY AND EQUALITY

Despite its fragmentations and displacements, then, 'the self' does relate to a real set of histories. But what are the 'real histories' to which so many at this conference have 'owned up'? How new is this new condition? It does seem that more and more people now recognize themselves in the narratives of displacement. But the narratives of displacement have certain conditions of existence, real histories in the contemporary world, which are not only or exclusively psychical, not simply 'journeys of the mind'. What is that special moment? Is it simply the recognition of a general condition of fragmentation at the end of the twentieth century?

It may be true that the self is always, in a sense, a fiction, just as the kinds of 'closures' that are required to create communities of identification—nation, ethnic group, families, sexualities, et cetera—are arbitrary closures; and the forms of political action, whether movements, or parties, or classes, those too, are temporary, partial, arbitrary. I believe it is an immensely important gain when one recognizes that all identity is constructed across difference and begins to live with the politics of difference. But doesn't the acceptance of the fictional or narrative status of identity in relation to the world also require, as a necessity, its opposite —the moment of arbitrary closure? Is it possible for there to be action or identity in the world without arbitrary closure—what one might call the necessity to meaning of the end of the sentence? Potentially, discourse is endless: the infinite semiosis of meaning. But to say anything at all in particular, you do have to stop talking. Of course, every full stop is provisional. The next sentence will take nearly all of it back. So what is this 'ending'? It's a kind of stake, a kind of wager. It says, 'I need to say something, something... just now.' It is not forever, not totally universally true. It is not underpinned by any infinite guarantees. But just now, this is what I mean; this is who I am. At a certain point, in a certain discourse we call these unfinished closures, 'the self', 'society', 'politics', et cetera. Full stop. OK. There really (as they say) is no full stop of that kind. Politics, without the arbitrary interposition of power in language, the cut of ideology, the positioning, the crossing of lines, the rupture, is impossible. I don't understand political action without that moment. I don't see where it comes from. I don't see how it is possible. All the social movements that have tried to transform society and have required the constitution of new subjectivities have had to accept the necessarily fictional, but also the fictional necessity, of the arbitrary closure which is not the end, but which makes both politics and identity possible.

Now I perfectly recognize that this recognition of difference, of the impossibility of 'identity' in its fully unified meaning, does, of course, transform our sense of what politics is about. It transforms the nature of political commitment. Hundred-and-one percent commitment is no longer possible. But the politics of infinitely advancing while looking over the shoulder is a very dangerous exercise. You tend to fall into a hole. Is it possible, acknowledging the discourse of self-reflexivity, to constitute a *politics* in the recognition of the necessarily fictional nature of the modern self, and the necessary arbitrariness of the closure around the imaginary communities in relation to which we are constantly in the process of becoming 'selves'?

Looking at new conceptions of identity requires us also to look at re-definitions of the forms of politics following from that: the politics of difference, the politics of self-reflexivity, a politics that is open to contingency but still able to act.

The politics of infinite dispersal is the politics of
no action at all; and one can get into that from the
best of all possible motives (i.e., from the highest
of all possible intellectual abstractions). So one
has to reckon with the consequences of where that
absolutist discourse of postmodernism is pushing
one. Now, it seems to me that it is possible to think
about the nature of new political identities, which
isn't founded on the notion of some absolute,
integral self and which clearly can't arise from some
fully closed narrative of the self. A politics that
accepts the 'no necessary or essential correspond-
ence' of anything with anything, and there has to
be *a politics of articulation*—politics as a hegemonic
project.

I also believe that out there other identities
do matter. They're not the same as my inner space,
but I'm in some relationship, some dialogue, with
them. They are points of resistance to the solipsism
of much postmodernist discourse. I have to deal
with them, somehow. And all of that constitutes,
yes, a politics, in the general sense, a politics of
constituting 'unities'-in-difference. I think that
is a new conception of politics, rooted in a new
conception of the self, of identity. But I do think,
theoretically and intellectually, it requires us to
begin, not only to speak the language of dispersal,
but also the language of, as it were, contingent
closures of articulation.

You see, I don't think it's true that we've been
driven back to a definition of identity as the 'minimal
self'. Yes, it's true that the 'grand narratives' that
constituted the language of the self as an integral
entity don't hold. But actually, you know, it isn't
just the 'minimal selves' stalking out there with
absolutely no relation to one another. Let's think
about the question of nation and nationalism. One

is aware of the degree to which nationalism was/is constituted as one of those major poles or terrains of articulation of the self. I think it is very important how some people now (and I think particularly of the colonized subject) begin to reach for a new conception of ethnicity as a kind of counter to the old discourses of nationalism or national identity.

Now one knows these are dangerously overlapping terrains. All the same they are not identical. Ethnicity *can* be a constitutive element in the most viciously regressive kind of nationalism or national identity. But in our times, as an imaginary community, it is also beginning to carry some other meanings, and to define a new space for identity. It insists on difference—on the fact that every identity is placed, positioned, in a culture, a language, a history. Every statement comes from somewhere, from somebody in particular. It insists on specificity, on conjuncture. But it is not necessarily armour-plated against other identities. It is not tied to fixed, permanent, unalterable oppositions. It is not wholly defined by exclusion.

I don't want to present this new ethnicity as a powerless, perfect universe. Like all terrains of identification, it has dimensions of power in it. But it isn't quite so framed by those extremities of power and aggression, violence and mobilization, as the older forms of nationalism. The slow contradictory movement from 'nationalism' to 'ethnicity' as a source of identities is part of a new politics. It is also part of the 'decline of the West'—that immense process of historical relativization which is just to make the British, at least, feel just marginally 'marginal'.

This text was first published in Homi K. Bhabha, et al., eds., *Identity: The Real Me: Post-Modernism and the Question of Identity*, Identity Documents 6, (London, 1987), pp. 44-46.

I – DIVERSITY AND EQUALITY

Stuart Hall

Minimal Selves

1 — DIVERSITY AND EQUALITY

BECOMING-WORLD
A New Perspective on European Citizenship

Rosi Braidotti

1 – DIVERSITY AND EQUALITY

POLITICS OF LOCATION

We need to re-invent cosmopolitan citizenship for the twenty-first century, in a manner that moves beyond a-historical Eurocentrism on the one hand and a flat repetition of universalism on the other. It is time to embrace complexity, accountability, and solidarity with both human and non-human others, so as to 'become-world' together. In order to construct this new kind of cosmopolitan—or rather planetary— relations, we first need to do some serious critical thinking and work together to develop adequate understandings of our locations.

Becoming-world means creating a cosmo-politan bond among humans and non-humans as well, as I will argue in the second half of this essay. In order to reconstruct a cosmopolitan bond among ourselves, it is useful to start with a comprehensive analysis of our specific locations, our relationship to the social and ecological environments, our sense of genealogy, of intellectual and historical traditions. Locations are spatial-temporal coordinates that pro-vide the framework to analyze our existence in terms of space, that is to say: class, ethnicity, geopolitical relations, territorial and environmental belonging, nationality, and so on. But locations also define us in terms of time, that is to say by a sense of historical memory, family and personal genealogies, the attach-ment to religious and cultural practices, and trans-historical narratives. My model for this approach is the feminist method of the 'politics of location'. This is an empirical, embodied philosophy first developed by Simone de Beauvoir ([1949] 1973), to study the different experiences of women—as compared to men—in a patriarchal system. Assuming that women occupy a different location, and that this difference is a mark of inequality, de Beauvoir focused on the specific aspects of the social, mental, and emotional existence of what she named 'the second sex'.

The second feminist wave of the 1960s and 1970s in the USA expanded this method and Adrienne Rich actually coined the term 'politics of location' (Rich, 1987), as a way of accounting for diversity among different kinds of women unified within the generic category of gender. Differences of class, race, sexuality, ethnicity, religion, age, and ability fragment the unified gender category of 'woman' and add both depth and complexity to a feminist understanding of what it means to be a woman.

This insight was further developed into the cornerstone of feminist-situated epistemologies, also known as situated knowledge (Harding, 1986; Haraway, 1988). Applied in a broader sense to the construction of all subjects of knowledge, as an analytical tool, the politics of location and a situated knowledge provides the means to explore our respective locations and thus confront our differences critically. As a creative tool, it helps us mediate the tensions and conflicts emerging from the different locations and supports the construction of shareable discourses and practices. The focus on collaboration and sharing sustains the project of experimenting with ways of transforming the patterns of our social interaction, so as to increase our capacity to relate productively to each other. Awareness of the relational ties that bind us can help us devise ways of honouring them. In this regard we are better off replacing universalism with the recognition of interdependence, which in turn entails the mutual acceptance of the fact that the politics of location offer a pluralistic array of partial and hence limited perspectives.

The politics of location and situated knowledge are a way to explore and analyze the kinds and the degrees of difference, in terms of access and entitlements to power, without dialectical opposition and violence. This method aims at achieving accountability by unveiling the power locations that one inevitably inhabits as the site of one's social and subject-positions. I take power not as an exclusively negative term, but also as a productive one—it is both restrictive (*potestas*) and empowering or affirmative (*potentia*). The method of the politics of location and situated knowledge have enabled me to theorize the *nomadic* nature of subjectivity (Braidotti, 1994 and 2011). Subjectivity is nomadic, because of the multiple—and potentially contradictory—locations and power-relations that 'we' inhabit. The key idea is that each of us is not one closed and solid entity, but an open, relational, and multi-layered one. For example, 'we' can belong to multiple cultural communities that may not always be in harmonious terms or completely translatable into each other, and yet 'we' can find margins of encounter and negotiations between them. Similarly, 'we' are perfectly capable of speaking many languages, have family and friends in several countries, and yet be socialized adequately and function perfectly well. I have put 'we' deliberately in inverted commas to suspend any sense of self-evidence about this complex and internally fractured entity.

The point of complicating this subject position—'we'—is to shift the question of citizenship to a matter of shared values and active participation, while diffusing any kind of essentialized identity. Citizens are as citizens do; 'citizen acts' are their defining feature (Isin and Nielsen, 2008). This perspective offers an alternative to a sacralized notion of nationalism. Whether 'we' hold one nationality, or more than one, or whether 'we' are seeking a new nationality through migration, asylum, and human rights laws, 'we' are capable of behaving like responsible citizens. 'We' are not one and the same, the differences between us are sharp and often painful, but 'we' can act as subjects-in-becoming.

Being a nomadic subject means to understand that we belong, but that we also flow, because the boundaries between our different cultural locations are porous and not rigid.

The idea of nomadic subjectivity calls for an ethics of mutual respect. If we agree that locations are historicized and situated, but also dynamic foundations that structure one's being-in-the-world and one's social modes of belonging, it follows that they differ in quantitative and qualitative degrees. Whether we are diasporic, nomadic, hybrid, post-colonial, a migrant, a refugee, a post-communist, or an in-between subject, makes quite a difference. These positions are not the same, though they can be equivalent. The task of the critical thinker is to make relevant distinctions among these different locations and map their points of intersection, in order to create a politically invested account of our respective locations. I call this philosophical method of mapping the nomadic subject a 'cartography' (Braidotti, 2002). Such cartographies need to do justice to the power differentials involved in the different locations, while identifying a common project that can be shared by multiply-located subjects, committed to constructing new kinds of active citizenship.

The cartographic method of the politics of location can easily be applied to the analysis of other categories of nomadic subjectivity, for instance what it means to be human in the age of Artificial Intelligence and genomics; or what it means to speak of sustainability in the era known as the Anthropocene.[1] When we start from the relational nature of the subject and emphasize the

1   The term 'Anthropocene', coined in 2002 by Nobel Prize winner Paul J. Crutzen, describes the current geological era as dominated by measurable negative human impact on the Earth, through technological interventions and consumerism. It was officially adopted by the International Geological Congress in August 2016.

I — DIVERSITY AND EQUALITY

relation to others as constitutional of the self, the complications increase and multiply. The 'others' of the humans today are not only other human beings—anthropomorphic like ourselves, but differentiated—dialectically and hence negatively, by processes of sexualization, racialization, and ecologization (Braidotti, 2002). The non-human others include both organic non-humans such as animals, plants, bacteria, cells, et cetera, and technological non-human others, such as codes, networks, devices, and the like. This post-anthropocentric shift of today calls for a posthuman approach (Braidotti, 2013), to strike new modes of relation between human and non-human agents. In order to do justice to the complexity of our times, we need to think seriously about where 'we' all fit in between the Fourth Industrial Revolution (Schwab, 2015) and the Sixth Extinction (Kolbert, 2014). This challenge also complicates the task of thinking about the collective entity—'we'—that now must encompass not only anthropomorphic beings but also other species and the technological apparatus.

Over the last forty years, gender and post-colonial studies have taught us to analyze difference with higher degrees of subtlety. Thus, they argue that these 'others' are constitutive of the self, in that they are the specular opposite of the subject of modernity. Sexualized (women and LGBTQ+), racialized (the non-Europeans, blacks, indigenous, colonized others), and the ecologized others (the environment) are different-from, and hence worth-less-than 'Man'—the white, heterosexual, middle-class, urbanized, male. They function consequently as the negative complement of the dominant vision of the subject, which defines other categories oppositionally and organizes them through a hierarchical system. In fact, the superiority of the dominant subject position is registered in its ability to position the others as inferior. Dominant positions assert their dominance by indexing and policing access to and participation in system of entitlements and power. Thus, it is not because he is more rational that 'Man' is dominant, but rather that, being dominant, male subjectivity has monopolized rationality as his distinctive prerogative (Lloyd, 1985). The dominant subject defines himself as much by what he excludes—the 'others'—as by what he *in*cludes in his self-understanding. Moreover, the dominant subject is always presented as a natural necessity, or as the outcome of an unavoidable evolutionary effort, which allows it to function as the standard-bearer of successful normality. The natura-lization of power is one of the assets of dominant categories.

Because of the systemic way in which power works, as both entrapment and empowerment, we need critical and creative accounts of our multiple and potentially contradictory locations. Accepting that 'we' are in *this* predicament together, but 'we' are not one and the same is the first move towards a new vision of becoming-world, by which I mean a planetary citizenship that might be attuned to the complexity of our era.

Accepting that 'we' is not a universalist entity blurring all differences, but rather a relational threshold that acknowledges and honours those differences, is at the core of relational ethics. It combines the recognition that 'we' are fractured by multiple and multi-layered differences of locations, and hence of power and entitlements, with the rejection of a dialectical and negative view of these differences. Instead, differences become the building blocks of a shared sense of identity, while maintaining the diversity of situated locations and power relations that have structured the different kinds of subjects 'we' have become. To achieve this balancing act, 'we' have to produce a courageous act of collective creation of citizens that are rooted, yet flow, and that have left behind some of the more selfish aspects of liberal individualism, to recognize the active intervention of others in every aspect of our existence.

A POST-NATIONALIST EUROPEAN SPACE

If we now transpose my cartographic and nomadic approach to a changing European landscape, a number of interesting ideas emerge on how to go beyond methodological nationalism (Beck, 2007) and develop a transformative European citizenship for the third millennium. A new agenda needs to be set, which is no longer that of a Eurocentric identity, but rather a serious transformation of it, towards an open and relational 'we' as situated yet different citizens in a fast-changing world. Eurocentrism is an old-fashioned but powerful habit of thought that supports a flattering rendition of 'Europeanness' as a civilizational marker. This attitude transforms Europe from a concrete geopolitical location with a specific history, into an abstract and value-laden ideal. Europe as the symbol of rational self-consciousness posits itself as a special site of scientific reason and cultural genius and as the motor of world-historical progress towards modernity. We need to replace this imperial vision with something more grounded, less pretentious and better attuned to a shared planetary condition that 'we' all share in—although we are not one and the same.

The fundamental question today is not just who we *are*, but rather what we are capable of *becoming*. In an age that is marked by many forms of social and political regression, notably the rise of new forms of nationalism, populism, and neo-fascist and undemocratic movements, we need to develop forms of shared responsibility for the specific location that is Europe. These regressive attitudes must be transformed collectively and give way to the affirmative transformations I outlined before: a becoming-world in a relational and productive manner. Symbolic of the regressive tendencies in Europe at present is the deterioration of our collective relationship to migrants, refugees, and asylum-seekers, who bear the brunt of racism in contemporary Europe, as the project of multiculturalism seems to have lost momentum.

Applying the method of the feminist politics of location to this conjuncture, we need to start the process by producing adequate understanding of our current situation. A useful first step is to remember our complex history, which is not only full of glorious achievement, but also of objectionable events and shameful moments. Europe's history includes colonialism, fascism, several world wars, and a tendency to xenophobic rejection of others. As Balibar (2001) and Bauman (2004) have argued, contemporary European subjects and citizens must meet the ethical obligation to be accountable for their past history and the long shadow it casts on present-day social and political life. This is the only way to avoid repeating the mistakes of the past. The new mission that Europe has to embrace is indeed courageous as well as creative. It entails the criticism of narrow-minded self-interests, intolerance, and racist rejection of otherness. We need to infuse new collective meaning and credible energy into the statement that 'we' are in *this* together. The sense of connection and cohesion needs to be qualified by the recognition of the structural differences of location that compose each of us. Only a grounded and accountable analysis of these differences in a non-oppositional manner can result in a renewed claim to community and belonging by singular subjects. This results in a proliferation of locally situated claims, or 'a collaborative morality' (Lloyd, 1996, p. 74).

This kind of situated 'becoming-world' has emerged as a powerful ethical claim in the work of post-colonial and race theorists, for instance in Edouard Glissant's idea of the poetics—as well as the politics—of relations (1990). Building on Stuart Hall's work, the notion of a 'planetary' connection that transcends the limitations of mere economic globalization is also gathering force. This can be seen in, for example, Paul Gilroy's concept of planetary cosmopolitanism (2000), Avtar Brah's diasporic ethics (1996), and Vandana Shiva's critique of 'bio-piracy' and capitalist de-humanization (1997). These positions, all other differences notwithstanding, produce alternative locations and figurations of what it means to be citizen today, enlarging narrow individualism and defying xenophobic reflexes. They not only emphasize hybridity, nomadism, multi-culturalism, diasporas, and creolization processes, but also work on building relational ties across these different locations. They transpose them into means of re-grounding connections and alliances among subjects marked by the diversity and the specificity of their respective ecologies of belonging. Nationalism and Eurocentrism are of hindrance, rather than assistance, in trying to redefine the planetary and interconnected nature of contemporary subjects. Together, 'we' need to raise the courage needed to move beyond these obstacles and adopt a more constructive approach.

No notion is more contested in European politics and social theory, especially in these days of Brexit and populist referenda, than the social-political project of the European Union (EU). As a mainstream project, the EU is a massive global economic and political player, but there is more to it than an aggressive concept of 'civilization'. As a transformative project, the EU constitutes the possibility of an alternative to the polarized social-economic realities of the global market and also as a progressive advocate of human rights and world peace. The EU is a multi-faceted political project, where reactionary and progressive elements of the European projects stand alongside one another. On the one hand, Europe celebrates its cultural diversity and the importance of transnational exchanges, but on the other hand it witnesses the resurgence of hyper-nationalisms occurring at the micro-level of regions, provinces, and even towns. The cosmopolitan global city and the paranoid Fortress Europe stand back-to-back as opposite but interconnected sides of the same coin.

In an attempt to bypass these binary oppositions, I emphasize an alternative vision of Europe as becoming-post-Eurocentric, or 'becoming-world'. The demise of Eurocentrism is taken as a generative premise that points to the possibility of a qualitative shift in our collective sense of identity and our collective imagining (Gatens and Lloyd, 1999). Contained within the progressive project of the EU are the seeds for a post-nationalist social-political space (Habermas, 2001). But this potential flies in the face of the insurgent neo-nationalism of European nation states, especially in the former East, which creates deep fissions within the EU. We then see how the sense of shared locations, of a common European citizenship and a shared history, culture, and currency, coexists with increasing internal fragmentation, regionalism, and xenophobia. The 'new' Europe is trying to steer its course in the midst of these complex and contradictory coordinates.

Again, let us take our history seriously. Since the end of European hegemony and especially after World War II, the decline of Europe as an imperial world power has been at the centre of the project of European unification. This means Europe has to find another way of being in the world.

A post-war consensus has arisen, which stresses the advantages of transforming Europe into a social-political laboratory so as to develop a post-nationalist sense of citizenship. Europe needs to become the place that is capable of elaborating a critical reflection on its own history, so as not to repeat its mistakes, notably the reduction of the different lives of sexualized, racialized, ecologized 'others' to a pejorative, devalorized status.

In my transformative perspective, the political project of European unification involves a qualitative shift in consciousness, which is the result of the process of analyzing and accounting for the politics of location. A courageous and creative post-nationalist vision of Europe entails the critique of ethnocentrism and of the self-appointed role of Europe as the alleged centre of the world—this false universalism underpinning the old Eurocentric identity. As an alternative, I propose a nomadic, that is to say multi-lingual, multi-faceted, and hybrid vision of Europe as a place where we are historically pushed to think about our history in a critical but also creative manner. As a post-nationalist project, the EU will, ideally, undergo a change in consciousness away from nationalism, moving towards a flexible mode of citizenship that allows for multiple belongings. This image of Europe is the opposite of the grandiose and aggressive universalism of the past. In contrast, this new image of Europe is both a situated and accountable perspective, that becomes-world in a non-conquering manner, turns our collective social imaginary away from the mental habit of cultural homogeneity towards a relational sense of diversity. Such a qualitative shift will allow us to look to the future confidently and to the past without nostalgia. As such it is a creative gesture, producing horizons of hope and, simultaneously, constructing the possibility of a future that is alive to the positivity of difference, the wealth of diversity, and the need for qualitative transformations.

For people who inhabit the European region, the present is marked to an unprecedented degree by trans-culturality, migration, and flows of migrants, itinerant workers, war refugees, and asylum seekers. The endless talk of yet another 'refugee crisis' is the symptom of the seabed change that is taking place in the very structure of European self-perception, as well as Europeans' anxiety about how to cope with this change. These new social-political realities raise fundamental questions concerning entitlement and agency. Thus the EU is faced with the following issue: can one be European, Black, Jewish, and Muslim? How can 'we', in all fairness, expect some of our fellow citizens to put up with being a Europe-born non-European, confined to the status of a second-class citizen within the dominant polity, while being an official citizen, as is often the case with generations of migrants and post-colonial citizens? Can the European project enable a new practice of flexible and multi-layered post-nationalist European subjectivity? Being a nomadic European subject means to be in transit within different identity-formations, but also to be sufficiently anchored to a historical position so as to accept responsibility for the location one occupies. By assuming full responsibility for the partial perspective of its own location, the European space can open up to a world no longer dominated by European power alone, while remaining loyal to the wealth and diversity of its roots.

The process of multiple belongings and a becoming-world of European citizens is transformative and affirmative, but not without its challenges. It requires some degree of dis-identification from established, nation-bound parameters of identity-formation. Such an enterprise inevitably entails a sense of loss as cherished habits of thought and representation will be left behind. This mature and sobering experience offers unquestionable benefits, because it produces a more adequate cartography of our real-life conditions, free from delusions of grandeur. It is therefore more lucid epistemologically and ethically fairer.

There is a lot to be learned from migrants, exiles, and refugees, who have first-hand experience of the pain and loss felt as a result of being uprooted and of forced dis-identification with familiar identities. Multi-locality is the affirmative translation of this negative sense of loss, allowing for the active production of multiple forms of belonging and complex allegiances (Glissant, 1997). What is lost with the sense of fixed origins is gained in an increased desire for multiple belonging.

The qualitative leap through the sense of loss of familiar values can turn into a gesture of active creation, one that affirms new ways of belonging. It is a fundamental reconfiguration of our way of being in the world that acknowledges the pain of loss whilst moving beyond it. Given that identifications constitute an inner scaffolding that supports one's sense of identity, we cannot shift the social imaginary lightly, like casting away a used garment. This process is difficult and more akin to shedding an old skin. Moreover, it is a collective activity; a group project that connects active, conscious, and willing citizens. It points towards a virtual, but no less real, destination —a post-nationalist Europe that becomes world. It is historically grounded, socially embedded, and already partly actualized in the joint endeavours of those who are currently working towards it. Affirming new ways of belonging mobilizes positive affects, such as creativity, the imagination, the power of vision and bonding.

Collectively, we can enlist the transformative power of these affective forces to create alternatives and move towards becoming-world. European post-nationalist or nomadic identity is such a project: political at heart, it has a strong ethical pull made up of conviction, vision, and desire. As a project it requires active participation and a striving towards what we are capable of becoming and different ways of inhabiting the European social space.

Far from being the prelude to a neo-universal stance, or its dialectical pluralist counterpart, or even the relativistic acceptance of all and any locations, the project of the becoming-world of Europe is an ethical transformation by a former centre that chooses the path of immanent change and multi-layered transformation. 'We' need to collectively produce enough self-respect and visionary energy to shed nationalism and become the subjects of multiple ecologies of belonging. The key here is an ethics of respect for diversity that produces mutually interdependent nomadic subjects and thus constitutes communities across multiple locations and generations. This humble project of being worthy of the present world while also resisting it, aims at constructing together social horizons of hope and sustainability. It expresses a transformative talent, that is to say a commonly shared commitment to social infrastructures of generosity, which might enable 'us' to be affirmative in this becoming-world together.

LITERATURE

Balibar, Etienne. *Nous, Citoyens de l'Europe? Les Frontiers, l'Etat, le People*. Paris, 2001.

Bauman, Zygmunt. *Europe, an Unfinished Adventure*. Cambridge, 2004.

Beauvoir, Simone de. *The Second Sex*. New York, [1949] 1973.

Beck, Ulrich. 'The Cosmopolitan Condition: Why Methodological Nationalism Fails.' *Theory, Culture and Society* 24, no. 7/8 (2007), pp. 286–290.

Brah, Avtar. *Cartographies of Diaspora—Contesting Identities*. London and New York, 1996.

Braidotti, Rosi. *Patterns of Dissonance*. Cambridge, 1991.

Braidotti, Rosi. *Nomadic Subjects*. New York, 1994 and 2011 (2nd ed.).

Braidotti, Rosi. *Metamorphoses. Towards a Materialist Theory of Becoming*. Cambridge, 2002.

Braidotti, Rosi. *Transpositions: On Nomadic Ethics*. Cambridge, 2006.

Braidotti, Rosi. *The Posthuman*. Cambridge, 2013.

Deleuze, Gilles, and Felix Guattari. *A Thousand Plateaus: Capitalism and Schizophrenia*. Minneapolis, 1987.

Deleuze, Gilles. *Spinoza: Practical Philosophy*. San Francisco, 1988.

Gatens, Moira, and Genevieve Lloyd. *Collective Imaginings*. New York, 1999.

Gilroy, Paul. *Against Race: Imaging Political Culture Beyond the Colour Line*. Cambridge, 2000.

Glissant, Edouard. *Poetics of Relation*. Wing, Ann Arbor, 1997.

Habermas, Jurgen. *The Postnational Constellation*. Cambridge, MA, 2001.

Haraway, Donna. 'Situated Knowledges: The Science Question In Feminism as a Site of Discourse on the Privilege of Partial Perspective.' *Feminist Studies* 14, no. 3 (1988), pp. 575–599.

Harding, Sandra. *The Science Question in Feminism*. Ithaca, 1986.

Isin, Engin, and Greg M. Nielsen. *Acts of Citizenship*. London, 2008.

Kolbert, Elizabeth. *The Sixth Extinction*. New York, 2014.

Lloyd, Genevieve. *The Man of Reason: Male and Female in Western Philosophy*. London, 1985.

Lloyd, Genevieve. *Part of Nature: Self-knowledge in Spinoza's Ethic*. Ithaca, 1994.

Lloyd, Genevieve. *Spinoza and the Ethics*. New York, 1996.

Rich, Adrienne. *Blood, Bread and Poetry*. London, 1987.

Schwab, Klaus. 'The Fourth Industrial Revolution', *Foreign Affairs*, 12 December 2015.

Shiva, Vandana. *Biopiracy: The Plunder of Nature and Knowledge*. Boston, 1997.

1 – DIVERSITY AND EQUALITY

ART, KNOWLEDGE, AND POLITICS

Vasyl Cherepanyn
in conversation with Wietske Maas

1 — DIVERSITY AND EQUALITY

WIETSKE MAAS • You are Head of the Visual Culture Research Center (Kiev, Ukraine), the institutional organizer of The School of Kyiv—Kyiv Biennial 2015 as well as The Kyiv International—Kyiv Biennial 2017. VCRC was founded in 2008 at the National University of Kyiv-Mohyla Academy as a platform for collaboration between academics, artists, and activists. Can you tell us about those early days—what made you set up this collective? Why was it an important thing to do back then?

VASYL CHEREPANYN • It is perhaps not a coincidence that VCRC was set up by people that primarily came from the Cultural Studies Department. In 2008, Cultural Studies was still a relatively new discipline in Ukraine, and, even today, it still does not have a fully established position within academia. We felt the need to abandon the existing disciplinary boundaries between the fields of art, humanities, and politics. As the university bureaucracy did not allow for such an interdisciplinary approach, we came up with the idea to start our own centre to create a multifaceted environment that would contribute to the analysis of Ukraine's post-Soviet condition in terms of art, knowledge, and politics.

Besides the desire to create such a platform, there was also a more practical reason behind the decision to establish the centre: we simply needed a space. Not merely a small university room that would force us to develop our artistic and scholarly projects everywhere and nowhere. Since 1994, our university had been hosting the Soros Center for Contemporary Art—Kyiv, which was created with funding by Georges Soros as part of the international SCCA Network to support contemporary visual arts in Ukraine. Situated in a renovated eighteenth-century historical landmark building of the university, the SCCA—Kyiv was a unique spot on the Ukrainian art map. It invited internationally acclaimed artists such as Jannis Kounellis and Ilya Kabakov to develop projects specifically for the location. When the SCCA was forced to close in 2008, after Soros had already stopped financing it in the early 2000s, we decided to step in to save the space as a public platform for the integration of contemporary artistic practices and scientific disciplines within the academic field. In short, it provided us with the opportunity to mingle artistic and academic activities at one single spot.

This interdisciplinary approach, which was much informed by Cultural Studies, was rather new in the Ukrainian context and it has greatly defined the way we work up until today. In fact, the premises that we have inhabited since then are all a kind of 'transformer spaces', not simply places for the conducting of seminars and art performances alike, but spaces that have exhibitions as research-based knowledge, in which researchers and artists can speak out as activists. It was precisely this combination of approaches that proved to be particularly fruitful, but at the same time our achievements—coupled with the fact that we were basically operating as a political organization within the university system—gradually led to a direct confrontation with the university authorities. In the four years that we were there, we actually organized more international events than the university in its entirety had done since its foundation in the early 1990s. In a way, VCRC had become a university within the university. In 2012 we finally left after the university's management had decided to censor and shut down the 'Ukrainian Body' exhibition because of what it deemed to be obscene content.

WM • As you know, Stuart Hall, the inaugural ECF Princess Margriet Award for Culture laureate was a leading figure in giving shape and substance to the field of Cultural Studies examining how culture can tell us something about the world that the traditional disciplines of politics or economics alone could not. Culture, said Hall, works by indirection. It is a kind of 'knowledge' that teaches us how to listen and look. As Hall said in his laudation speech: 'It learns through the body, as well as the mind and the intellect. Its terrain is that of the imagination.' You already mentioned that Cultural Studies greatly informed VCRC and its activities. How did VCRC as an organization develop further the tools it learned from Cultural Studies in light of the highly politicized context—then and now— in Ukraine?

VC • Cultural Studies was a relatively new discipline at the time and even today it is still marked by a rich variation of approaches throughout Ukrainian academia. While at some universities the focus was on ethnology or rather ethnography, almost in a nineteenth-century style, at our institute this flexibility was taken as an opportunity to adopt a more modern, twentieth-century approach, more or less in keeping with what in the United States is called Social Anthropology. In fact, considering the important originating role (neo-)Marxism has played in the development of Cultural Studies, in Great Britain and elsewhere, we were constantly thinking of setting up what might be called 'Social-Cultural Studies'.

Although our approach was more in tune with recent developments in the field, I had the feeling that concepts such as race, gender, and class were still not sufficiently discussed throughout our university. In my view this was all the more remarkable given the highly politicized situation. Because these notions and tools were not structurally available within the university itself, VCRC tried to fill this gap by becoming not only a site of knowledge production but also one of knowledge transmission, a platform where both cultural and educational activities took place. The centre offered me the freedom to develop my own curriculum, which in turn allowed me to transmit precisely the kinds of notions that had been developed by scholars such as Hall.

Even though I had the feeling that my teaching had an amazing effect on progress, I still felt that it was not enough, that I was only influencing my own students without really affecting changes on a societal level. I strongly believed that there was a more general need for instruments with which to influence the larger context and to change the status quo, not only as an individual person, but also as a collective subject. It is within this context and for this reason that this 'politicization of cultural critical thinking' somehow took place. While the tools developed within the Cultural Studies discipline were still something of a novelty in the post-Soviet context, VCRC was instrumental in transmitting this type of knowledge. We need to remember that before the launch of VCRC, lectures about politically involved or socially engaged notions or ideas were considered to be rather radical, almost alien. In that sense, one might perhaps even say that—within the Ukrainian context—we brought culture into conversation with politics.

WM • This brings me to the question of how VCRC politcizes culture rather than culturalizes (if that is a word!) politics. The cultural work you are doing is with the aim of constructing political language (and a political subjectivity) differently. Culture contributes to creating what Stuart Hall has called a new 'terrain of imagination', on which a more socially just politics must form. Yet does this run the risk of being perceived as using culture for political ends as well? What I want to ask is: What do you see as different about politicized culture (which enacts other possible futures) rather than being at the service of already extant political imaginary?

VC • A question that is often posed by thinkers and theoreticians today is: What can art and culture do to change politics and to increase political participation? Likewise, many people are now turning to culture instead of politics in search for answers. In my opinion, this redirection from politics to culture actually diverts our attention from the real social and political problems that we are facing. It is highly problematic in the sense that it relegates culture to the position of a mere signifier or symptom of the current political crisis. The politicization of the notion of multiculturalism is but one example of this type of redirection. The basic problem with such a politicization of culture is that it can actually be used for diametrically opposed political objectives. The important question to ask should therefore not be what culture can do to change the current status quo, but what we can do to reaffirm, reinstate, and reconstitute political participation.

In trying to come up with new ways with which to tackle this problem, VCRC based itself in the tradition of the so-called engaged intelligentsia, a notion that in the Ukrainian and broader—Eastern European—context can be traced back to the nineteenth century. This notion revolves around the idea that the cultural, academic, and political fields, rather than distinct categories, are much more intertwined and funda-mentally share the same approach. Notwithstanding the methodological differences between them and the different types of media in which they are represented, they can all equally contribute to social and political change. It is also for this reason that we adopted 'art, knowledge, politics' as our unofficial motto. In my view, the fences that exist or are being put up between these fields in our society today are obsolete and do not make any sense.

Art, knowledge, and politics all participate in the search for a new political subjectivity. In response to the current falsification and degradation of both culture and education by the current ideological order in Ukraine—that is, a mixture between neo-liberalism and a kind of post-Soviet neo-feudalism, we have tried to construct new social ties between these fields and to develop new types of education, including self-edu-cation. Both culture and education are stages for social learning and in that respect are revolutionary as such. Seen from this perspective, the adding of a cultural and educational component to politics is highly important. In fact, without a cultural or educational component, there is the danger that the political and ideological outcome of a revolution will be the exact opposite of what it originally set out to achieve. We have seen this happening in the aftermath of the occupation of Maidan Square and what happened with the progressive demands that were made. The uprising presented an emergent horizon of a new collective political subjectivity, but this new 'terrain of the imagination' was short-lived, and the forces of the revolution were turned against itself, became diverted into a counter-revolution against a large part of what it initially stood for.

> WM • From education as social learning, I would like to shift to the notion of politics of difference and identity in the Ukrainian context. In 'Minimal Selves' (see elsewhere in this part of the book) Stuart Hall has spoken about how identity is always, in a sense, a fiction: 'Identity is formed in that unstable point where the unspeakable stories of subjectivity meet the narratives of history, of a culture.' For Hall, this impossibility of a fully resolved identity also transforms our sense of what politics is about: '… toward a politics of difference, a politics of self-reflexivity, a politics that is open to contingency but is still able to act.' I am wondering how you see this politics of difference—without easy transfer of generalizations—and how this could translate to the contemporary condition in Ukraine?

VC • Ukraine is a very strong example of this identitarian type of politics, which is unfortunately very typical of the political situation in many other European countries today. Identity, identitarian politics, and the politics of difference are of course very difficult subjects. There seems always to have been a tendency to perceive identity as a fixed entity. Nowadays the notion of a 'politics of difference' is very popular among social and political scientists, but in practice it has always failed to materialize. That is probably also what Stuart Hall was referring to when he said that identity is a fiction and that a fully resolved identity will always remain an impossibility. Nonetheless, in Ukraine and elsewhere in Europe we can still detect a stubborn search for such fully resolved identities. In my opinion, this is a very dangerous road to take and I don't think that I am exaggerating when I say that it can only lead us directly into the concentration camps. In other words, this leaves us with a virtually unresolvable dilemma: how to construct a new narrative in which identity is a fiction but at the same time can still be taken as a point of reference?

Considering this fictional nature and its capacity to be multi-layered, I believe that practically, politically, and philosophically speaking it would be much better not to focus too much on the issue of identity and instead to return to the philosophical notion of subjectivity, a concept that has unfortunately been more less abandoned since the days when Foucault and others were talking about it. In my opinion, the great value of returning to the notion of subjectivity—both in philosophical and political terms—lies herein that in doing so we also are immediately reinstating and emphasizing the existence of 'truth'. Today it is often remarked that we are living in a post-truth world. But I would rather say that we are currently living in a pre-truth world—a world in which the truth has not arrived yet. However, truth certainly does exist.

We should not confuse this notion of truth in one's subjectivity with the pseudo-liberal idea that currently dominates our society according to which 'truth' is an *objective* idea. The search for subjectivity is important because it is all about freedom. It is what a truly emancipated, democratic, and grassroots political practice looks like. Recently we have seen the emergence of a variety of protest movements—Occupy, the Arab Spring, and Maidan—which seem to be reflective of a widespread search for a new political subjectivity. I think that here in Ukraine we could detect a similar pursuit for a political subjectivity that might eventually result in a more just and democratic society.

WM • One of the principles of VCRC's work is its specificity to the Ukrainian context on the one hand and its European and international interrelatedness on the other. I would like to mention here Rosi Braidotti's concept of transformative European citizenship, which in her view should be a nomadic, non-static one that cannot be achieved without historical consciousness. However, 'this continent has chosen amnesia and oblivion; the negation of its own history', she says, resulting in 'the poverty of the European imaginary'. (A negation of the anti-fascist thoughts that were the founding thoughts of a united Europe). How would you reflect on this lack of historical memory that is required to unhinge citizenship from national identities and identitarian subjects?

VC • Like Braidotti, I believe that it is possible to dislodge citizenship from national identities. Also, in this case there are perhaps no ready-made recipes available to us, but there are at least a number of historical examples that suggest that it can be realized. While our current understanding of the notion of citizenship may be said to have derived from that developed within the Roman Empire, the very idea that people from various backgrounds (geographical, ethnic, religious or otherwise) could be part of one and the same citizenry—quite revolutionary back then—would now virtually be unthinkable.

There are some lessons to be learned from the past, but in order to be able to remove national identities from citizenship, we should perhaps first stop with being so obsessed with the memory issue. Somewhere along the line we forgot about the future. Today we are always paying attention to and trying to play out our emotions through the politics of memory. I think that our obsession with the past is actually one of the outcomes of the identitarian politics that we were talking about. By now it has become a standard practice of reactionary groups and populism throughout the world. A good example is Donald Trump's famous slogan: 'Make America Great Again!' What does he really mean when he says 'again'? Does he mean that we need to go back to the 1930s, the 1950s or the 1960s? That is exactly the problem, that this 'again' has never existed. This memory, or this supposedly lost past that identity is trying to re-establish, is just a fake one.

I also agree with Braidotti that Europe today suffers from amnesia and oblivion and has lost its historical consciousness. Even the very recent past seems to have been forgotten. It is really unbelievable that people nowadays are either not aware or even consciously negate the central role that anti-fascist thoughts have played in the creation of the European Union. It is astonishing to see that throughout Europe fascism has returned as a sub-culture, perhaps using a slightly different vocabulary than before—now with an anti-migrant lexicon—but playing the same game all over again. What is more, it is not only fascist groups that negate history, also state authorities are now playing with that. We are really entering dark times, and it has only just started.

> WM • 'Visual culture' is pivotal to the name of your organization. In a highly mediated reality—one imbricated by warfare and a war on truth and remembering—we are bombarded with a barrage of visual narratives that give us all but fragmentary or distorted impressions. How, in this struggle for reality (and, as you point out, for a new political subjectivity), can visual culture equip us with the ability to learn and respond otherwise?

VC • What is important here is the dialectical approach, involving a range of disciplines that are on the edge of contemporary knowledge production, such as image studies, media, history of art, classical aesthetics, and so on. It is an anthropological type of knowledge, which therefore makes it very political. But also, from an institutional perspective, visual culture here refers to the strategies of visualizing the invisible. We have always tried to follow this line of thinking and to articulate issues that are normally being silenced, for whatever reasons. I think that the political or ideological task of visual culture, as a field of research, is exactly that: to make the invisible visible, to bring it to the conscious level. This is rooted in the tradition of the philosophy of suspicion. But at the same time, it also has, and needs, a very artistic and aesthetical dimension.

With respect to the war on truth and remembering, in Ukraine, right now we witness a war on imagery, basically destroying all the imagery that we inherited from the Soviet times, including the Ukrainian avant-garde modernist heritage. Unfortunately there is no differentiated thinking and the problem with that is that we are giving up our own subjective-becoming. Whether people like it or not, Ukrainian modernism was part of the Soviet modernism, which was part of European modernism. It is a shame that this heritage is partly forgotten and partly destroyed.

We have to remember that the Russian military invasion and occupation of the Ukrainian territories is not just the whole story about this war, seen from the Kremlin side. This war has been conducted on the screens, which is usually called propaganda, but it's rather a new type of media war. Globally as well, we are living in times when different kinds of occupants or terrorists, be it state actors, or pseudo state organizations like Daesh are using aesthetical visual methods in order to present themselves. So we see that artists or cultural actors nowadays feel that they are deprived of their own methods. I see it as a very important challenge for visual culture as a field how to counter the fact that reactionary and counter-revolutionary forces throughout the world, nowadays are using the same type of imagery or even the same visuality as cultural actors and artist. The struggle for reality is taking place in the field of visual culture: it is channelling populist approaches, but at the same time it proposes and opens new emancipated possibilities.

WM • The School of Kyiv—Kyiv Biennial 2015 had a strong emphasis on the notion of learning,

I – DIVERSITY AND EQUALITY

on art as education, and on acknowledging wounds and traumas specific to the Ukrainian context. The Kyiv International—Kyiv Biennial 2017 was shaped as an 'international forum for art and knowledge' to expand the scope of arts and culture towards knowledge, critical theory, and politics. With regard to the last experiences of these Biennials, what have you learned as an organization, and what are the resonances both locally and further afield? Maybe thinking of some of the difficulties you have encountered that have led you to grow otherwise, or having to change yourself, organizationally.

VC • From the very beginning it was not our intention to do a Biennial as such. It was also not about making some big events only every two years. But we saw that using the format and framework of the Biennial in a different way helped to reform the whole notion of it. We see that in other places as well. The Biennials that are held today are totally different from what they used to be five or seven years ago. The most important thing for us, in that restructured format, is the possibility to have an umbrella under which we can involve other collective subjects, other institutions, on a more or less permanent basis. In this sense, the Kyiv Biennial became also an institutional extension of VCRC, a kind of artistic performance of the organization, and in this it is our medium. Using this format as an umbrella project gives us the possibility to have a multi-institutional kind of subjectivity. Similarly, you have the collective subjectivity of an organization in order to be able to do something that you wouldn't be able to do as a person. In the case of the Biennial, it provides the specific institutional setting that allows you to do much more internationally, than just being determined solely by your locality.

What was striking in comparing the two Biennials is the shift of attention on a European scale but also a changed environment within the Ukrainian context. In 2015, just after the Maidan protest that took place in 2013 and 2014, there was much international interest in The School of Kyiv—Kyiv Biennial 2015, in terms of support and participation from various European countries. But over time we came to understand to which extent we are shaped by the media field: as soon as Ukraine was out of media attention, it became less fashionable, less interesting… We immediately felt that in terms of response to the 2017 edition. Of course, in a way Ukraine has itself to blame for that, after doing nothing following Maidan. There were still some hopes for reforms in 2015, but in general they turned out to be very superficial. This trend is also taking place in other European countries, where we see more and more reactionary and authoritarian tendencies.

> WM • Has the way VCRC is being received changed in Kiev and further afield since the School of Kyiv?

VC • The authorities probably forgot that they took place, as they do not care much… As for the media field and the artistic circles of course, it gave us a specific shape, a kind of a trans-local skeleton. Both times we had this very important urban dimension where we left the university context and imposed the logic of the cultural field, and its institutional structure, on the city. Unfortunately, in the City of Kyiv, there is no institutionally protected space where you can be part of some knowledge and image production, in a critical way, so we tried to offer this space through the Biennials.

Unfortunately we also learned with whom not to collaborate. For the first Biennial in 2015, we approached a mix of institutions that we inherited from the Soviet times, newly emerged institutions with activist background that where set up after Maidan, official institutions such as art academies and museums, educational institutions like universities, some commercial galleries. So we worked with all varieties of institutional actors present in the city, but unfortunately most of them are not ready to sustain the proposed activities on the longer term. On the one hand, this institutional constellation in the city space was one of our biggest achievements after the School of Kyiv. But without a lot of support it is not sustainable—neither financially, nor institutionally, nor conceptually.

On the other hand, there is also a post-revolutionary trend in the Ukrainian context where more and more actors, people, and institutions are not interested in participating in something that may be perceived as non-patriotic by the media or the general public, that may create problems for them. And looking at the Kyiv International—Kyiv Biennial 2017, people sometimes thought that it was better not to be trapped in a situation with somebody who is problematic, who is already a target for some groups. In their view it is better to just skip it, and not be involved in something poten-tially scandalous. Generally, with the 2017 Biennial, we found ourselves in much more problematic and dangerous conditions.

WM • Let us conclude by looking towards the future, even though, as you already say, things are unfortunately becoming direr. With reference to the theme of the book, 'Courageous Citizens', and the potential of culture to enact social change, we also spoke with David Harvey about the need for citizens to keep on exercising democratic rights in their cities. In some regions of Europe, and the world, exercising these rights takes more courage than in others. Harvey stresses that we not only need courageous citizens, but savvy ones, people with knowledge who understand the underlying patterns behind the symptoms. This seems to us to be exactly what you're trying to do with the VCRC. However, you seem to need a good portion of fearlessness, as distinct from courage. You mentioned this also in your 2017 Biennial opening speech. What is it that makes you go on doing your important but very long-term oriented work? Things don't change overnight, as we know.

VC • I would not heroicize this fearlessness, or courage, because biographically-wise, you just don't know what comes next, and somehow you just do what seems to be the immediate task, in fact consisting of very peaceful activities, but at some point one understands that there is no other way out than doing just that. That somehow it would be even more dangerous to hide than to expose oneself publicly with this kind of activities. But also, politically, I think, it's a situation where we observe negative trends all around. In Ukraine, the revolutionary chance, which was a really huge and very powerful one, seems to be lost and to some extent, Europe is also moving in that direction.

The reactionary forces are taking power in more and more countries. All the revolutionary potential is substituted with warfare, and the war itself has become a norm of conducting politics today. So I think it is really a very depressing political landscape. At the same time, when you observe a variety of negative trends, then you just don't have another option than to be really radical. If you still see some positive agenda on the horizon, you can still keep some hope of moving there. But if there is no such kind of horizon, the only way out, the only option, is to just try to go on, even if you do not know what will happen—in a spirit of acceptance like in Nietzsche's Amor Fati: a large yes to the whole of life.

This is an edited version of a conversation between Vasyl Cherepanyn and Wietske Maas that took place in Amsterdam in January 2018.

77SQM_9:26MIN
Forensic Architecture

Shortly after 17:00 on 6 April 2006, Halit Yozgat, 21 years old, was murdered while attending the reception counter of his family-run Internet café in Kassel, Germany. His was the ninth of ten racist murders performed by a neo-Nazi group known as the National Socialist Underground (NSU) across Germany between 2000 and 2007.

Within the 77 square metres of the Internet café and the 9:26 minutes of the incident, different actors crossed paths—members of migrant communities, a state employee, and the murderers—and were architecturally disposed in relation to each other. The shop was thus a microcosm of the entire social and political controversy that makes the 'NSU Complex'.

In November 2016, eleven years after the murder, the citizens' and activist alliance 'Unraveling the NSU Complex', together with Haus der Kulturen der Welt (HKW), Initiative 6 April, and documenta 14 commissioned Forensic Architecture to investigate unresolved aspects of this crime. In addition to a written report, this resulted in a three-channel video installation presenting the results of the research, which was presented for the first time during documenta 14 in Kassel.

www.forensic-architecture.org/case/77sqm_926min/

Project team: Eyal Weizman (Principal Investigator), Christina Varvia (Project & Research Coordinator), Stefanos Levidis, Simone Rowat, Omar Ferwati, Nicholas Masterton, Yamen Albadin, Ortrun Bargholz, Eeva Sarlin, Bob Trafford, Franc Camps Febrer, Sarah Nankivell, Hana Rizvanolli, Chris Cobb Smith (Advisor), Lawrence abu Hamdan (Advisor)

Collaborators: Ayşe Güleç / Unraveling the NSU Complex, Initiative 6 April, and documenta 14; Natascha Sadr Haghighian / Unraveling the NSU Complex and Initiative 6 April; Fritz Laszlo Weber / Unraveling the NSU Complex, Initiative 6 April, and documenta 14; Cordula Hamschmidt / HKW; Khaled Abdulwahed; Cem Kayan; Vanina Vignal; Sebastian Bodirsky / Unraveling the NSU Complex; Dr. Salvador Navarro-Martinez / Imperial College London; Grant Waters / Anderson Acoustics; Armament Research Services (ARES); Mihai Meirosu / Nvision Audio; Christopher Hupe / HKW; Frank Bubenwer; Gozen Atila; Markus Mohr / Unraveling the NSU Complex; Mathias Zieske; Serdar Kazak / Unraveling the NSU Complex and Initiative 6 April; Norma Tiedemann; Basak Ertur

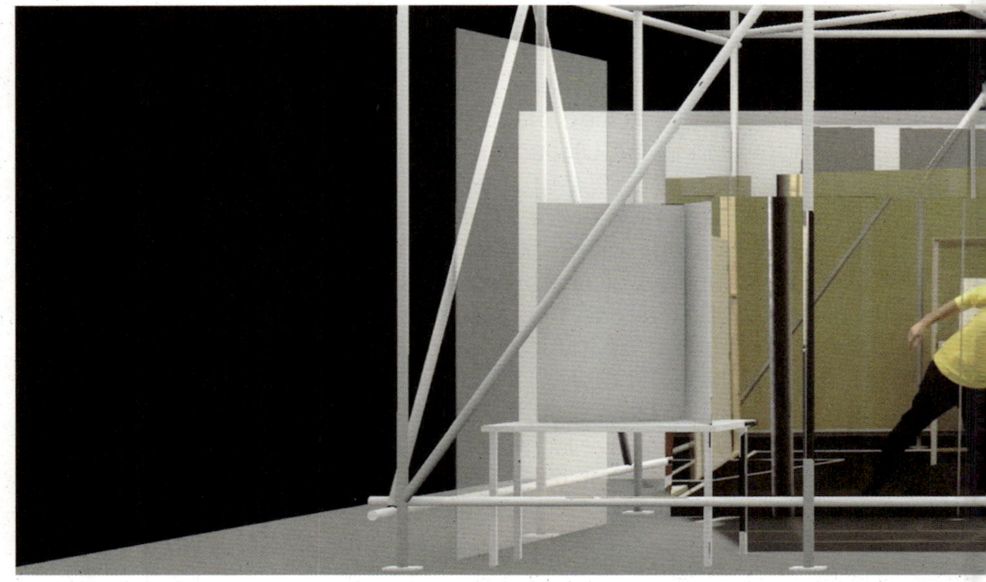

Composite of both the physical and virtual reconstructions of the internet cafe where Halit Yozgat was murdered on 6 April 2006 by a member of the neo-Nazi group known as the National Socialist Underground (NSU). Image: Forensic Architecture, 2017

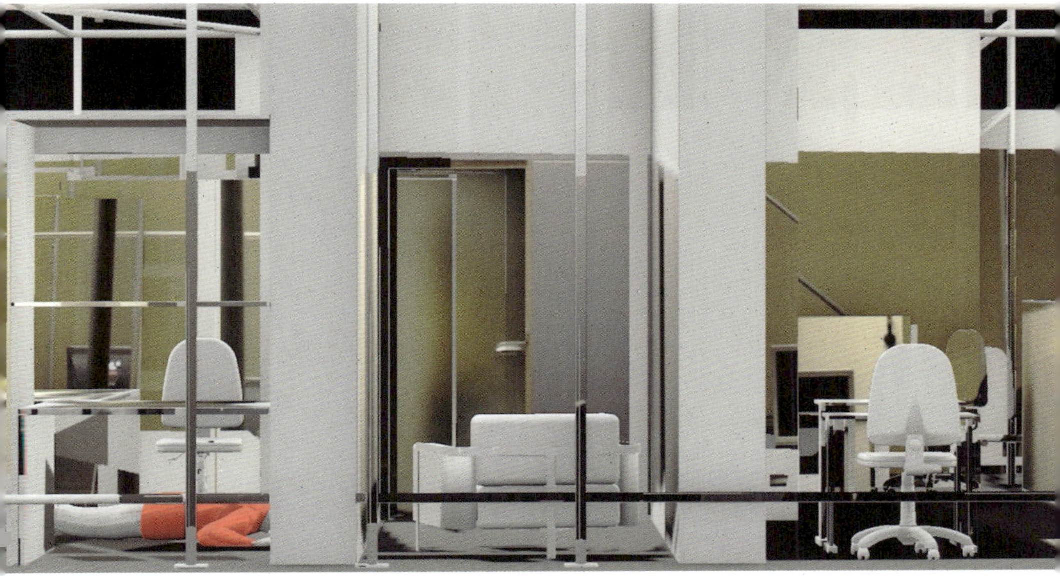

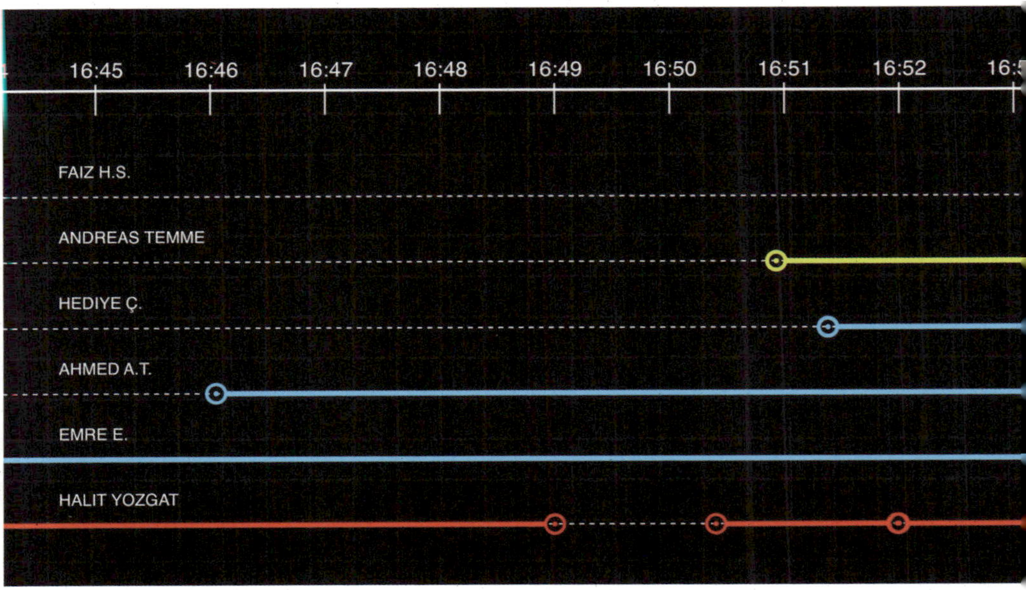

16:45
16:46
16:47
16:48
16:49
16:50
16:51
16:52
16:5
FAIZ H.S.
ANDREAS TEMME
HEDIYE Ç.
AHMED A.T.
EMRE E.
HALIT YOZGAT

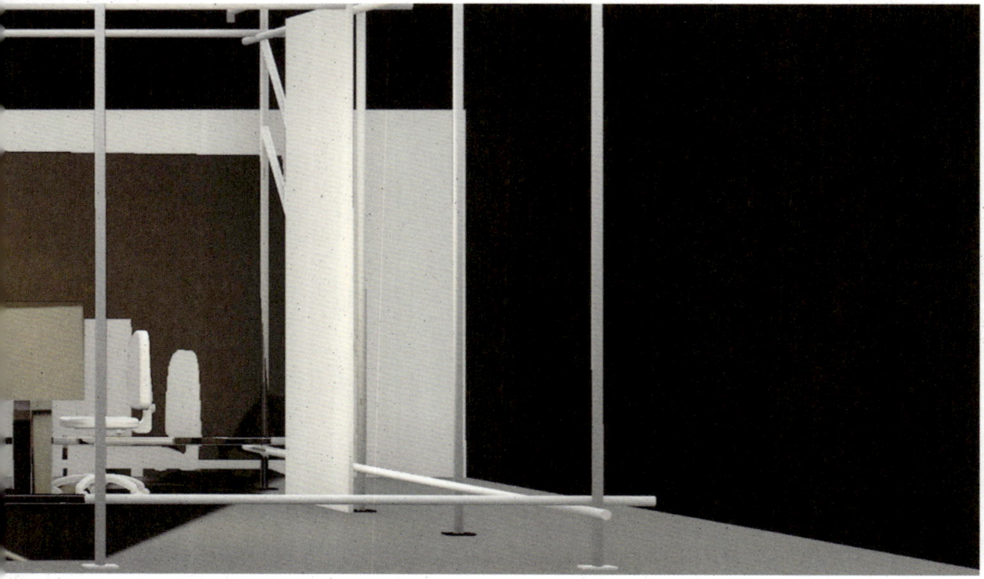

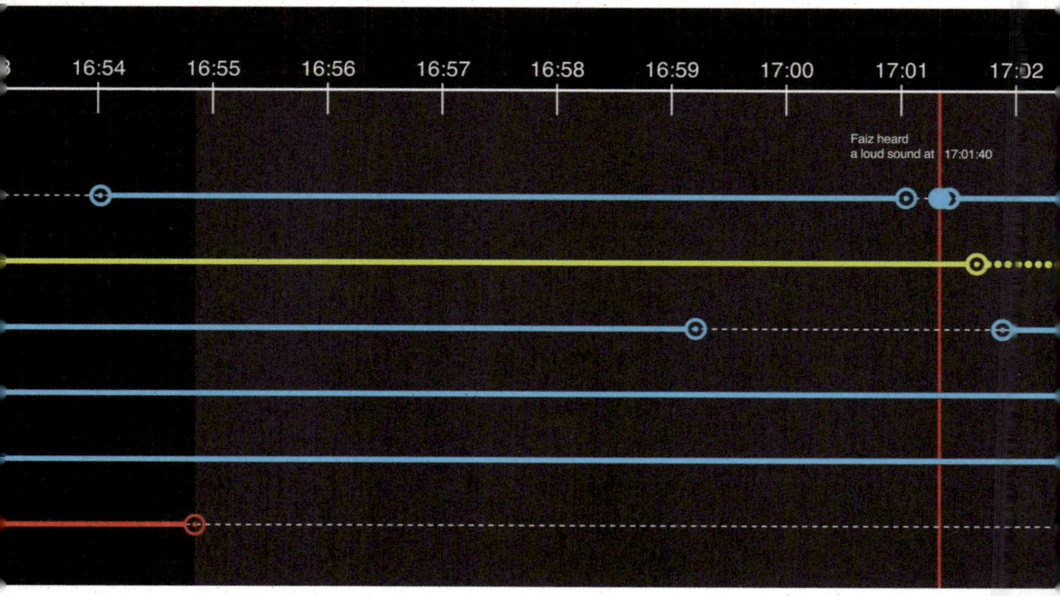

16:54 16:55 16:56 16:57 16:58 16:59 17:00 17:01 17:02

Faiz heard
a loud sound at 17:01:40

A timeline constructed based on computer and phone logs from the internet cafe plotting the incidents that unfolded over a period of 25 minutes surrounding the time of the murder of Halit Yozgat.
Image: Forensic Architecture, 2017

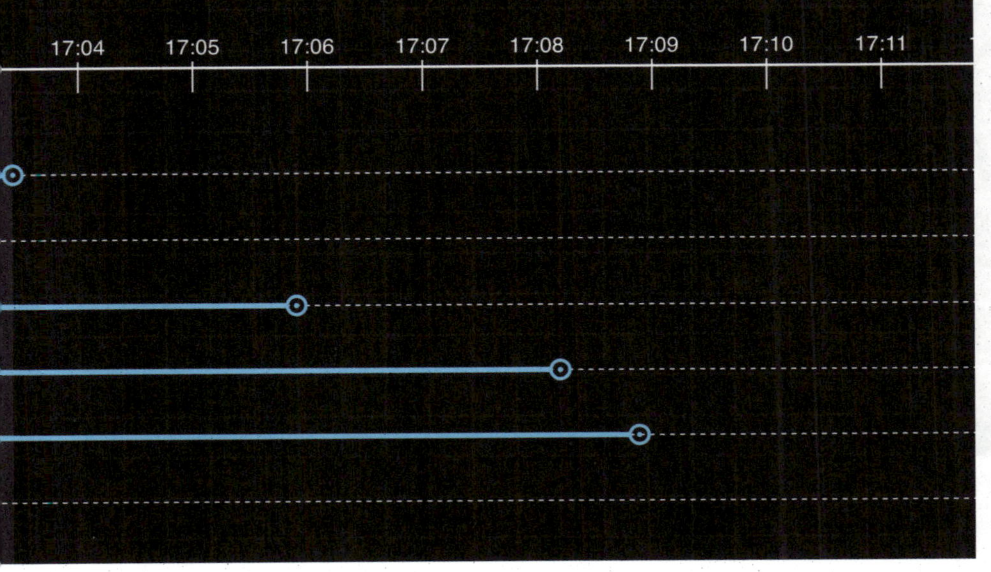

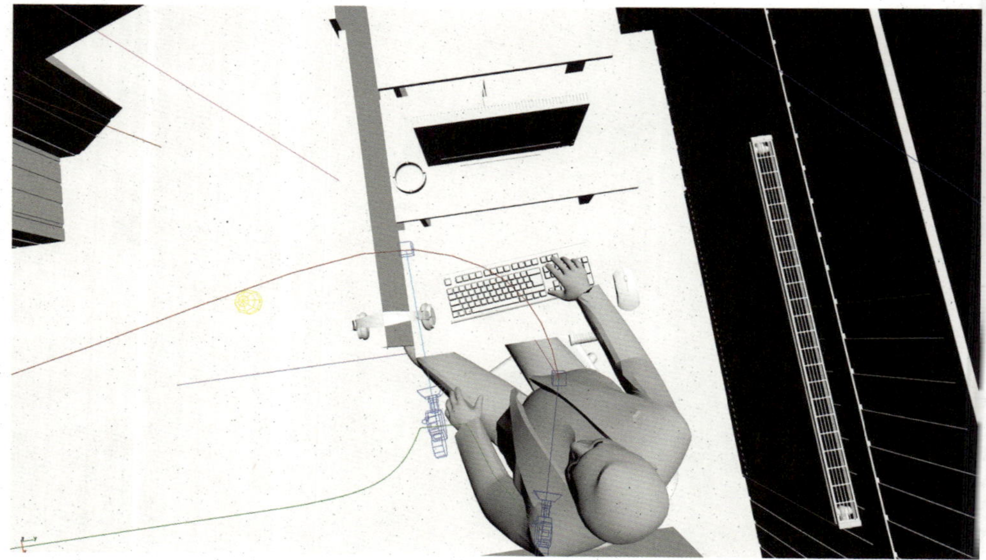

Computer simulation of motion tracking and vision simulation of the person
whose testimony is in doubt.
Image: Forensic Architecture, 2017

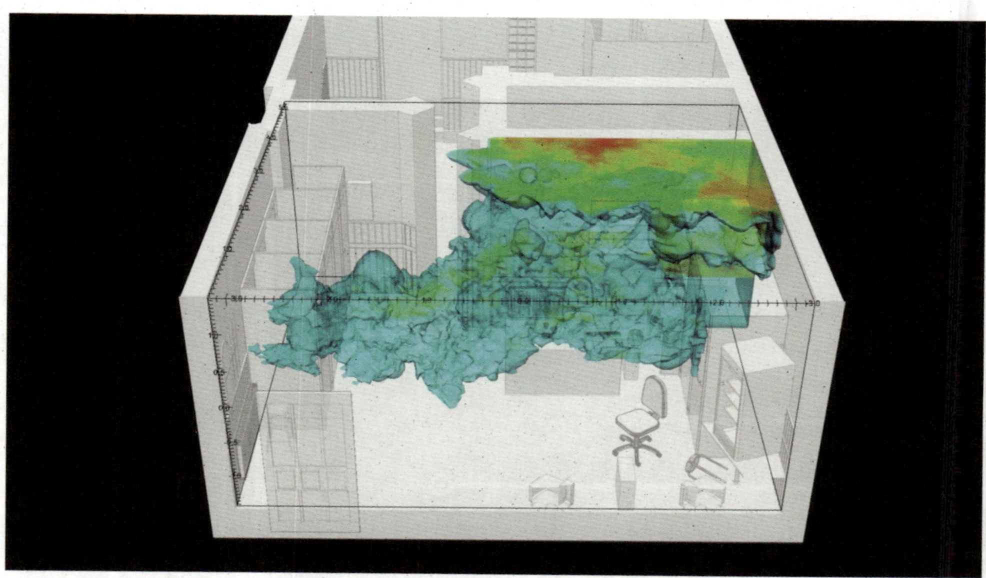

Simulation of the fluid dynamics of smell particles (ammonia) within the
front room of the internet cafe.
Image: Dr. Salvador Navarro-Martinez and Forensic Architecture, 2017

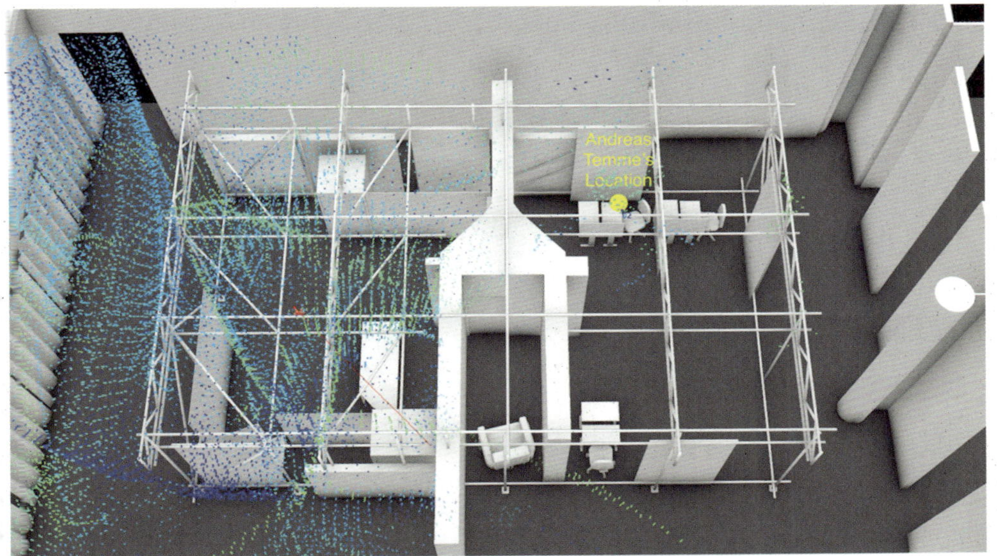

Simulated propagation of sound within a digital model of the internet café that
was designed to mimic the exact dimensions and materials of the actual space.
Image: Forensic Architecture and Anderson Acoustics, 2017

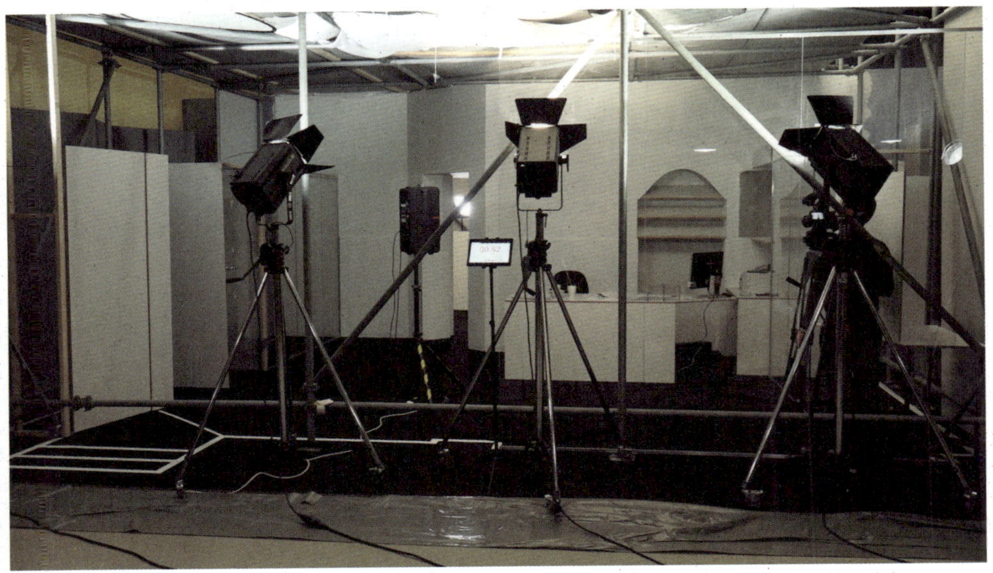

Full-scale mock up of the internet cafe at the House of World Cultures (HKW)
in Berlin, constructed between 6–11 March 2017.
Image: Forensic Architecture, 2017

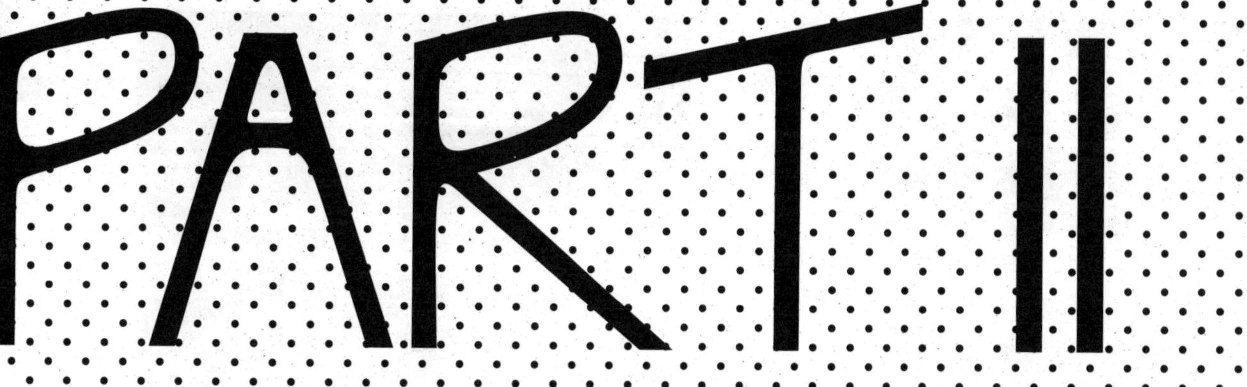

PART II

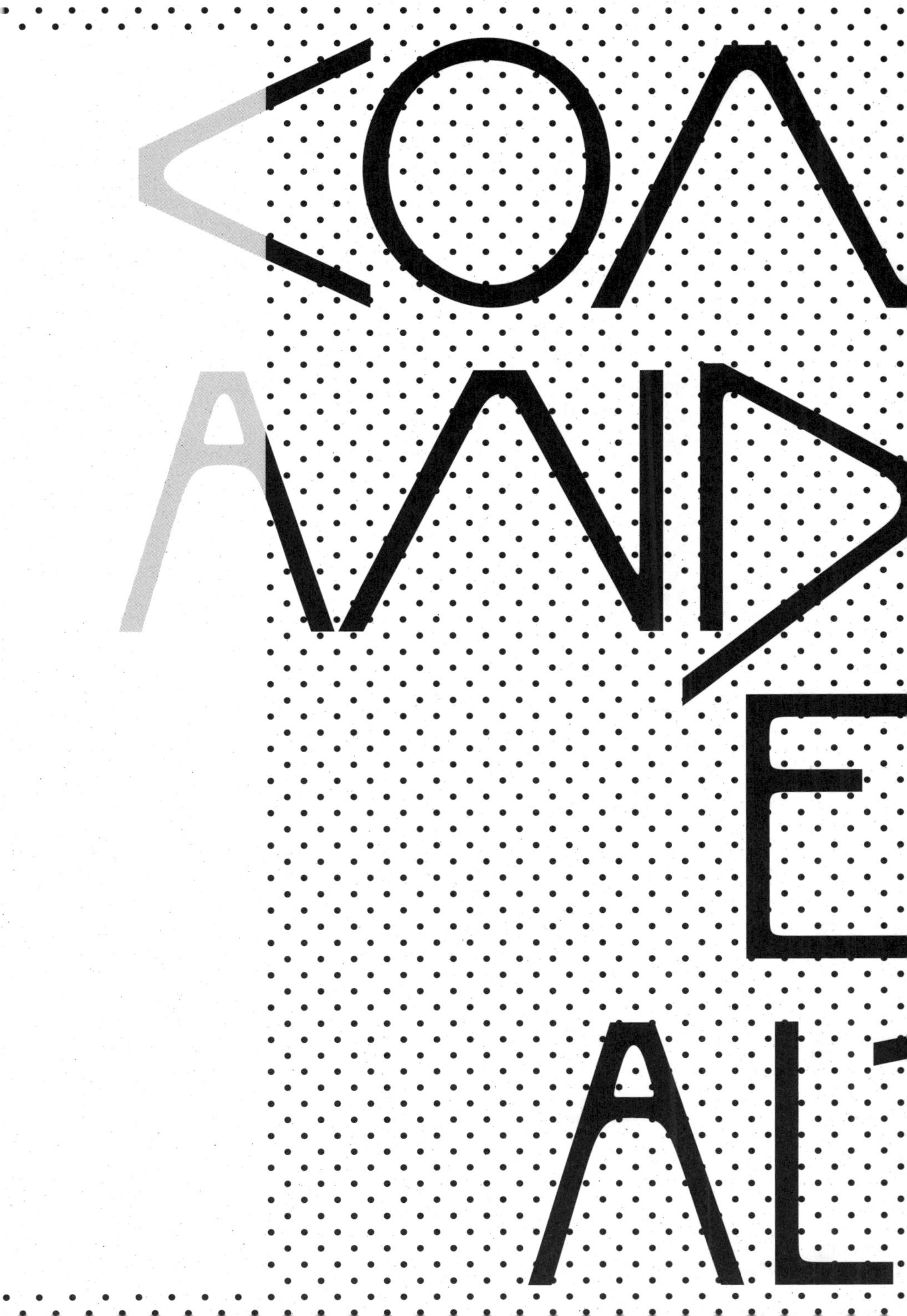

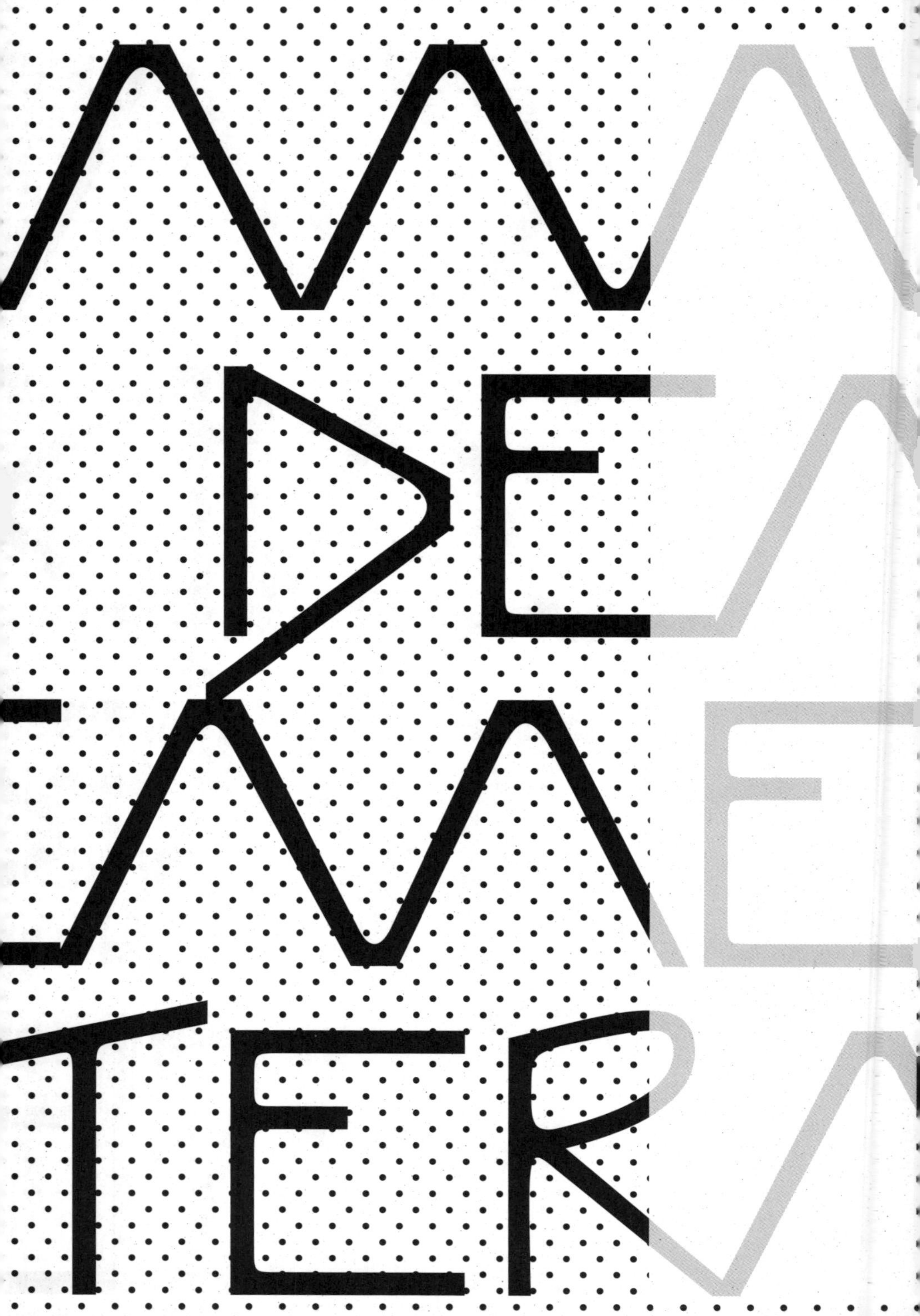

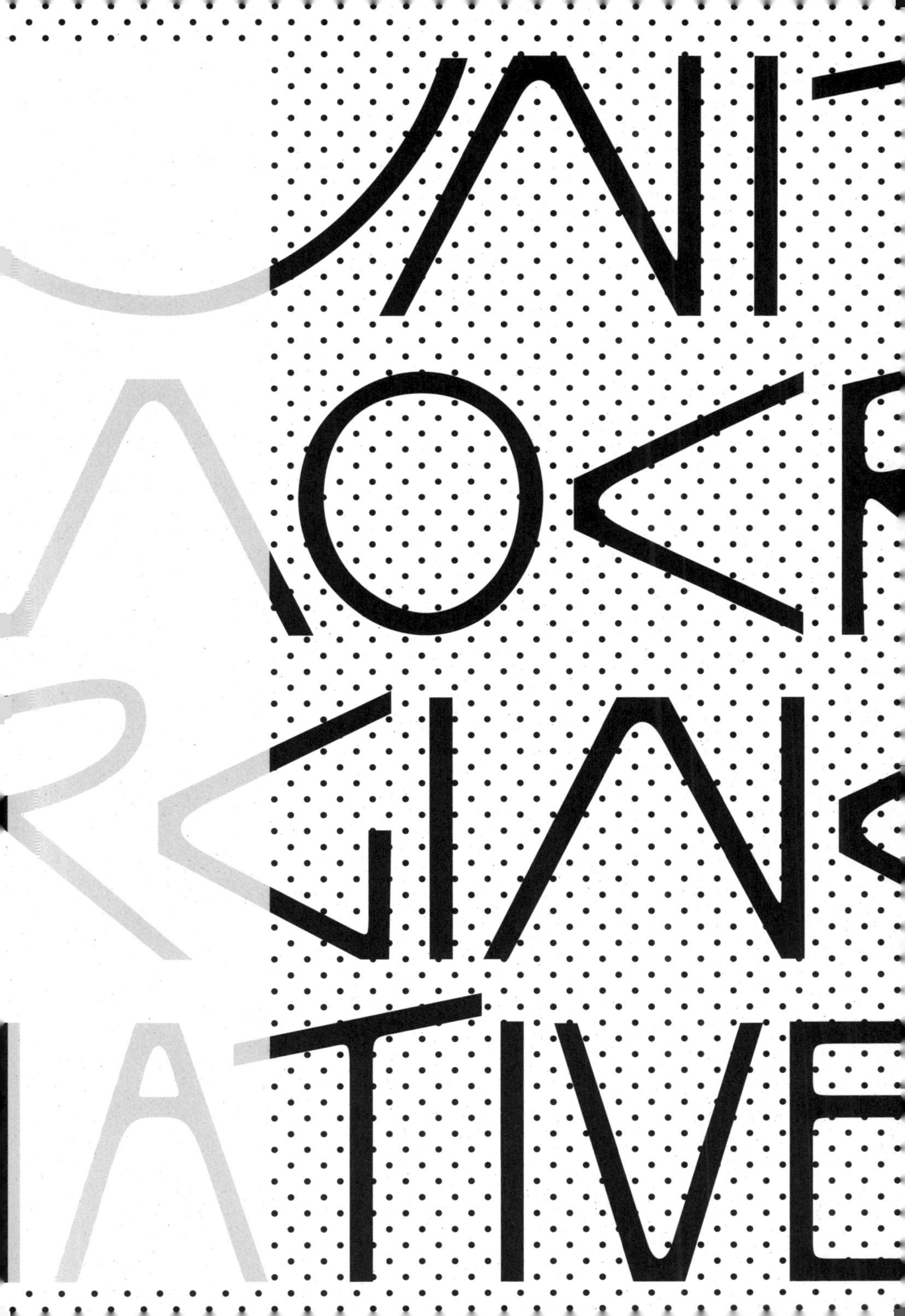

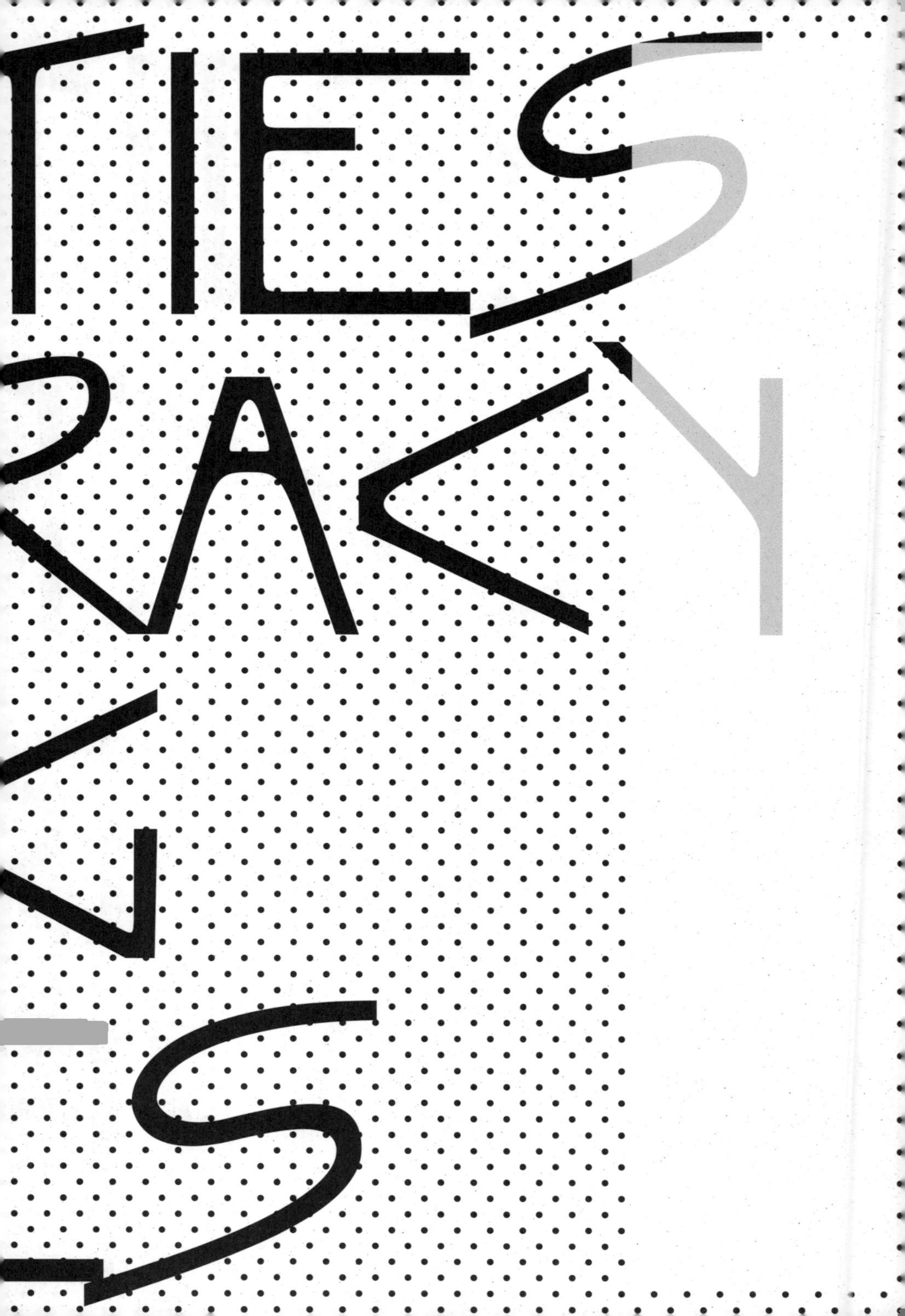

II – COMMUNITIES AND DEMOCRACY: EMERGING ALTERNATIVES

CULTURE, COMMONS, AND THE RIGHT TO THE CITY

David Harvey
in conversation with Wietske Maas

II – COMMUNITIES AND DEMOCRACY

WIETSKE MAAS • What, in your view, is the relation between grassroots urban movements and new projects such as Teatro Valle Occupato and Right to the City Zagreb, that experiment between traditional activism and the constituent process of building what they call the 'new institutions of the common'?

DAVID HARVEY • The kind of world we have built, particularly over the last thirty years has produced a situation of mass alienation. Most people do not have satisfying jobs anymore, most are routine, there is a sense of meaninglessness about what people do. Consumerism has been pushed, particularly for elite groups. We have on the one hand conspicuous consumption that looks like a cornucopia of desire, but you go out in the city and there are a mass of people living in conditions of poverty. So you have unmet needs on the one hand and conspicuous consumption on the other, which is producing what I call a mass alienation that attaches to contemporary consumerism. The power of traditional institutions to give voice to people's needs has also been eroded. Trust in the political process is at an all-time low.

As a result of this, many people feel alienated in their daily lives. There is a search for alternative meanings to those provided by the monetary calculus and simple economic value... so there is a search and a longing for an alternative value structure.

There are very conscious movements such as Teatro Valle Occupato and the Right to the City movement in Zagreb, in which Teodor Celakoski is a nodal figure, where there is a conscious search for new value forms and practices. In searching for something different, nobody is absolutely clear what these alternative values might look like. All we do know is that these values are not provided by the monetary calculus, they are not those provided by consumerism, but by neediness of people's lives as they search out cultural practices involving new ways of social relating, new ways of relating to nature, new urban environments and alternative forms of daily life.

So there is a great deal of experimentation going on with the daily life in the city. And that experimentation is backed by the idea of the right to the city, the feeling and the belief that we have a right to build cities in a different image, different to that which developers want and what the big financial institutions want. When you ask yourselves 'what kind of city do we want to live in?', that cannot be divorced from the issue of 'what kind of people do we want to be?' and 'how do we want to be?' And therefore it is a remaking of ourselves and a remaking of the world around us that go hand in hand. I think cultural projects are absolutely central to that exploration. Which is not to say that all cultural projects will arrive at a good answer because we do not know what the answer is. For this reason there has to be a lot of experimentation. The current proliferation of cultural projects must be supported and validated, because this is one of the ways we can explore the possibility of developing a rather different kind of world and alternative forms of value to those given in the monetary calculus.

WM • Culture can generate new values and new ways of relating socially, but what about the economic value culture is seen to generate? By expanding our imagination to think through alternatives, culture can play a role in thinking and enacting democracy differently, but what if we take into account the ambivalence of cultural production in relation to the economy of the city, such as cases of gentrification witnessed in many European cities (which you have also analyzed in your research on Barcelona)?

DH • Any project which you launch can always be co-opted by capital. We get a movement of say hip hop in the Bronx, which can be a vibrant expression of street culture, and immediately capital then capitalizes on it and starts to commercialize it. Over the last thirty years, capital has placed a particular emphasis on the so-called cultural industries as a vehicle for capital accumulation. This is a real problem because the cultural industries try to commodify many of the things I have been talking about. Some of the cultural producers are happy to be co-opted because they make some money and get a better living. Succumbing to that temptation is understandable for individuals but the collective effect can be disastrous.

    So there is a complicated relationship between the commercialization of cultural activities and the utilization of those cultural forms to gain monopoly dividends on the basis of the uniqueness and authenticity of what exists in some aspects of urban cultural life. The commodification of culture is part of the problem. But that commodification can be turned the other way if the cultural producers are keenly aware of the dangers. The commodification can be used to gain the necessary resources to explore alternatives even further. There is a dialectical relation between how capital tries to co-opt and commodify cultural activities and how cultural producers might be able to turn that around and use it in a different way to advance the cause of alternative modes of valuation. My own view is that there has been far too much 'museumification'. Every place is opening museums of everything. Some of it is not very helpful, but some of it can be appropriated by the cultural community in ways which are possibly progressive.

There is a dialectical relation; so yes there are traps and dangers which are attached to cultural industries being part of an economic development strategy that is associated with building museums, gentrification, 'Disneyfica-tion' of central cities turning them into pretty little places satisfying to the tourist gaze. As a result, many areas lose their character of being authentic public spaces for the people. They become bland homogenized spaces for the tourist trade. In New York City, for example, some of the spaces that acted as commons in the sense that they were spaces of natural assembly have been turned into nice little parks with flowerbeds you are not allowed to walk on. They have become controlled rather than free spaces when what you want from the standpoint of real development of urban life are spaces where things can happen, open to the politics of encounters that are not regulated by state or increasingly privatized powers (as in shopping malls).

I get very nervous when cities start emphasizing the development of cultural industries as being central to what their economic development strategy is. That is maybe the end of really vibrant street culture. There is an acute danger of that. At its worst, cultural industries and tourism can end up destroying the character of cities. Florence is a city that has been destroyed by tourism. It is interesting that in recent years anti-tourist movements have arisen in many European cities as residents seek to protect their particular identities and ways of life from barbaric forms of tourism.

WM • What can other European cities and movements learn from the experiment of 'commoning' launched by Teatro Valle Occupato in Rome? How can this new form of cultural production, urban occupation, and constituent process be translated to a larger, European scale?

DH • We tend to think of the space of the city as being divided between public and private. We tend to have the view that public spaces are open to the public. But actually a lot of public spaces in the city are tightly regulated, tightly controlled and they are not open to the public at all. It therefore means that if I want access to some space, it is very difficult to find one. To give an example: if I want to hold a political meeting to have an assembly, if I try to do that in a public school in Manhattan, then I would have to go through the school board and they would want to know what the meeting is about. Almost certainly we would be denied the possibility of using that public space for a common purpose.

One of the curious things about the Occupy movement, is that Occupy could not find a public space either in London or New York City, so they occupied a private space. In London the only one they could find was on the steps of St Paul's Cathedral. If I wanted to have a meeting in New York City probably the best place I could go would be one of the churches, because very often they say 'well yeah, it's ok'. These days there is very little space for commoning—that is a spontaneous getting together. And we start to find all kinds of regulatory mechanisms. For instance, again in New York City there were bike-ins where cyclists would get together. They have now passed a law that if there are more than fifty bicycles on the street at the same time it is an illegal thing.

Actually opening public spaces so they become common spaces is a big political project. It means that you have to battle the state or private property to try and find a democratic space where you can have an assembly of some kind. What was so interesting about many of these movements that occurred in cities like in

Syntagma Square in Athens and the Puerta del Sol Square in Madrid is the way they turned a public space into a space of commoning. This happened in Tahir Square in Cairo too. A formal public space was turned into a space of commoning. But you see immediately that the authorities did not like that, they do not want the public space to be public in that way, they do not want it to be part of the commons. So I like to think of different property regimes: there is a state property regime, which is about public space, and there is a private property regime of exclusionary private spaces, but in between we need to build a common property regime to encourage democratic practices in the city and to encourage people to come together and discuss, debate, and decide on what shall or shall not happen in the city and how particular areas of the city can be redeveloped and used for the benefit of the people as a whole.

So having urban assemblies seems to me to be one of the democratic ways to go, but in order to have assemblies you need to have open spaces where you can easily assemble and we should have an automatic right to that. We should not always have to go to the public administration and beg for permission that is in any case so often denied. For instance, when there was a plan to have a protest in Central Park in New York City, we were told that we could not use Central Park because we might hurt the grass. The political rights of grass superseded the political rights of people! In many places, public space has been reengineered and exclusionary practices instituted in the name of counter-terrorism. Some of that may be necessary but we also desperately need to protect and encourage a tradition of commoning. The state should not be in a position to stop us exercising democratic rights within the urban environment.

WM • Do you see the practice of commoning as a third way between the state and the market? And can a wider movement of commoning be something that can discipline the state to change, to become more inclusive to the interests of a non-marketable commons?

DH • It is a third way, but you are not going to get that third way unless you have a popular disciplining of the state in terms of what the state is allowed to do and how the state is allowed to do it. There is going to have to be a broad base movement against the state regulation of the public spaces that says you cannot do this or cannot do that. I would like it if, for example, it was mandated that the public schools should always be open for use by the public for assembly purposes. You look at the city and you see all these public (state) spaces that are not open for public political purposes. Unfortunately, 'the threat of terrorism' has provided an excuse for the increasing securitization and militarization of public spaces. Consider the effect of all that close circuit television surveillance backed by facial recognition technology. We live in a society that is full of surveillance, and that is also highly regulated. We need democratically to break some of that down in order to liberate ourselves from a world of total regulation in both private and public spaces. We need to open a third space for commoning.

WM • In the past years, we have seen the rise of the so-called sharing economy (Uber, Lyft, Airbnb), digital platforms where everyone can become a supplier for all sorts of products and services. Yet, the notion of 'sharing' is a misnomer, as these digital platform companies function as monopolies that, in the absence of a physical infrastructure of their own, extract value from our labour, social relations, personal assets, and time. What kind of citizen engagement and imagination do we need to practice forms of social cooperation and justice to provide an alternative to such disruptive forms of platform capitalism?

DH • Cultural impulses travel widely across space and time. Capital has long taken advantage of this to commodify and sell imagery, exotica, even turning the daily news into some kind of reality show (the more gruesome the better, it often seems). International tourism—even when marketed as culturally and ecologically sensitive—is big business and market value is, as it were, constructed and extracted on a huge scale. But then think of the positive side of this. I always liked to ask the students in my beginning class in geography where their breakfasts came from. I wanted students to recognize the million and one threads that connect them to millions of people around the world, to recognize that cities, for example, are not discrete and isolated entities but nodal points in the midst of a variety of flows of goods, ideas, information, images, and the like. So it is not only capital that extracts value from all of this.

People can sense the necessity for an alternative politics, fight for economic justice for those who put breakfast on their table and find ways to link together socially and politically around an alternative idea of value. Look at the contagion effect of the Occupy movement or how an event like Gezi Park in Istanbul in 2013 spread to many other Turkish cities and may even have helped inspire the uprisings in Brazilian cities a few weeks later. Social media have been important to the Left as well as to the Right and to capital. The fight for social justice and the right to the city is not confined to one space.

WM • Can we say that the idea of people as citizens begins to devolve as the emphasis and ideal of entrepreneurial subjectivity increases?

DH • I am glad you ask this question because the question of political subjectivity is critical for understanding both the limits of and possibilities for radical action in our times. There are many—and I partly subscribe to this view myself—who see the rise of neoliberal forms of capitalism as both resting upon and promoting a subjectivity dominated by the entrepreneurialism in and of the self. The needy citizen is a bad citizen who deserves to be punished rather then helped (hence the punitive character of contemporary welfare arrangements in many states). We are invited to invest in ourselves and if we fail to invest in our own human capital then we deserve to fail. Neoliberalism is all about blaming the victim. But that is only part of the story. I mentioned at the start, the massive increase in alienation from work, from daily life, from sociality and politics. That is the underside of neoliberal political subjectivity and it leads to passive withdrawal, anger, and aggression that easily spills out into violence. Alienated populations can embrace right-wing populism, elect Donald Trump or support neo-fascist movements. The task for the Left is to channel alienation in another direction. This often means that those leftists who have invested in themselves through education, cultural activities and the like have to learn how to mobilize the bad and needy citizens to challenge the whole neoliberal system.

WM • And finally, where do you see the space, the possibility for citizenship in countries ruled by 'strong men' that are becoming more and more authoritarian, where what is 'regular' citizenship in one context becomes 'courageous' citizenship in another?

DH • One of the claims I made in 2005 with the publication of *A Brief History of Neoliberalism* was that the ideological justification and political legitimacy of the neoliberal project

would increasingly come into question. That
the contradiction between the supposed benefits
for the populace at large (as opposed to the top
one percent) and the realities of daily life would
become so severe that the only way the system
could be sustained would be by resorting to an
increasing authoritarianism of state power.
We have now clearly reached that stage. We can
and should struggle against the authoritarianism
and do everything we can to support those (as
in Turkey, for example) who are suffering most
severely from right-wing authoritarian populism.
But I also think it vital to recognize that at the
end of the day we need also to struggle against
the political-economic system that underpins
this shift to authoritarian right-wing politics.
We need not only courageous citizens, but
also savvy ones who see how capital's political
economy produces the alienation that gets
politically expressed through right-wing authoritarian political movements. The problem in the
United States is not only Donald Trump but
the political economic system and its alienations
that underpin his rise to power.

This is an edited version of a conversation between David Harvey and Wietske Maas that
took place in September 2013 at Teatro Valle Occupato and was revised and extended via
email in January 2018.

David Harvey

Culture, Commons, and the Right to the City

II – COMMUNITIES AND DEMOCRACY

THE GLOBAL CIVIL PARADE

Constitutions of Transnational Citizenship

Pascal Gielen

II – COMMUNITIES AND DEMOCRACY

CREEPING RAGE

Terrorist attacks and pervasive threats that hang over us today distract us from another kind of violence I want to discuss here. That violence includes a form of aggression that rather insidiously oozes throughout the world. Over the past decade we have been startled at intervals by sudden but intense outbursts of rage. The explanation for the kind of violence addressed here is not directly traceable to God or any particular country. That is why, like terrorism, it leads to as much incomprehension. Although sometimes their immediate cause can be identified, some of these eruptions—especially those of unusually large destructive proportions—are beyond any comprehension.

Whether it be riots in the *banlieues* of Paris, in the suburbs of London, in Brussels' Molenbeek district, the cat-and-mouse game around Antwerp's Turnhoutsebaan or the street violence in the Schilderswijk of The Hague, their cause is often ascribed to controversial arrests, or even fatal casualties caused by police violence. However, the reason why the reactions are so severe and why they also, quite massively, trigger a civic roar, remains unclear. Moreover, it can be particularly difficult to predict whether the dam is going to burst or whether there will be no eruption at all. In other words, while the symptoms are clear, the underlying disease remains elusive.

Surprised by a sudden eruption, the mainstream media and politicians have often proven to be lacking interpretive frameworks. At the time, Nicolas Sarkozy coined the phrase 'les racailles des banlieues' [the scum of the suburbs] while Dutch Prime Minister Mark Rutten talked about 'achterlijke gladiolen' [dim-witted morons]. When it happened in David Cameron's backyard, the former British Prime Minister struck a moralizing tone in saying, 'Young people and immigrants must urgently be re-taught the norms and values of their country.' In response to the riots on Turnhoutsebaan, the then Mayor of Antwerp abolished the city slogan 'The City is for Everyone'. From then on, the city was no longer for everyone.

Repressive measures such as zero tolerance and more police in the streets are accompanied by a strikingly moralizing rhetoric. Citizens must be re-taught norms and values, and those who refuse to change must relocate. The city and the country may indeed not be for just anyone anymore. Some people are just not worthy of being American, Belgian, British, German, Dutch, Russian or European. Their right to citizenship is, at the very least, doubtful.

The responses to these violent eruptions remind us that citizenship has always existed to create a regulatory mechanism of *inclusion and exclusion*. However, over the past decade we have been confronted with a notable shift in meaning, from a *formal* to a *moral* interpretation of the word: where the formal concept of citizenship concerns the legal status of a citizen, moral citizenship includes the extra-legal normative interpretation of what a good citizen is, or should be and should do. As the Dutch sociologist Willem Schinkel put it: 'Citizenship is a concept that will be stretched more and more in today's policy. The moral side of citizenship becomes the centre by emphasizing the formal aspects of citizenship. When "integration" is then seen as "citizenship", this will lead to a quasi-elimination of citizenship for many citizens in the formal sense. The state is trying to effect this by adapting the concept of citizenship to promote a discourse that makes clear who is and who is not part of the dream society.'[1]

ACTIVE CITIZENSHIP

As soon as emotions have cooled down and insults in the streets and the media have diminished, the view is cleared and there is room for more rational solutions, as in the 'motley crew' and their 'senseless' violence must be addressed proactively and more thoughtfully. In recent years, relief has also been sought in improved integration and participation policies. Every so often, the notions of 'active citizenship' and the 'participatory society' came to the fore. The 'Big Society' and active citizenship seemed to be David Cameron's panacea for social ailments such as violent outbursts.

But we also see these concepts emerge on a European level. *European citizenship* was first officially mentioned in the Treaty of Maastricht of 1992. The notion of active citizenship emerged again eight years later at the Lisbon Council of

1   Willem Schinkel, 'The Virtualization of Citizenship',
Critical Sociology 36, no. 2 (2010), pp. 265–283, p. 48.

Europe. There, citizenship was understood as a means of making Europe the most competitive and dynamic knowledge economy of the world.[2]

Over the past three decades, the mission of civic education has transformed the political landscape from one with a humanistic perspective (of learning how to be human) to one of learning how to be productive. In line with that, education is supposed to help people settle in the labour market. Thus, citizenship includes first and foremost a desire to integrate and participate in the economy. According to the Dutch pedagogue Gert Biesta, these terms of education lead to an interesting re-definition of civic rights and duties: 'Whereas in the past lifelong learning was an individual's right, which corresponded to the state's duty to provide resources and opportunities for lifelong learning, it seems that lifelong learning has increasingly become a duty for which individuals need to take responsibility, while it has become the right of the state to demand of all its citizens that they continuously engage in learning so as to keep up with the demands of the global economy.'[3]

THE PARTICIPATORY SOCIETY

A similar shift can be observed in the definition of *participation*. This concerns a shift in focus in policy from political participation to self-reliant participation.[4] The swing from the political to the moral dimension of citizenship implies both a politicization and an individualization. Thus, again we observe a return of the debate to the balance

2   Gert J.J. Biesta, *Learning Democracy in School and Society: Education, Lifelong Learning and the Politics of Citizenship* (Rotterdam, 2011), p. 34.
3   Ibid., pp. 66f.
4   Susan van Hees et al., 'Betekenissen van burgerschap van ouderen in de participatiesamenleving', *Tijdschrift Gezondheidswet* 93, no. 5 (2015), pp. 191–196, p. 192.

II – COMMUNITIES AND DEMOCRACY

of rights and obligations: the participation right of a citizen is renamed *a moral obligation*. At the same time, the legal-technical semantics around citizenship are sliding towards a rather affect-laden discourse. Herein, citizens are called upon to care for each other and be less dependent on the government.

The new politicized morality of affective citizenship focuses on the intimate local and affective relationships among citizens themselves, as opposed to the aloof national level and faceless bureaucracy of the welfare state. Moral and emotional ties thus receive more appreciation than legal-technical or political relationships. We see these personal and small dependencies in the return of terms such as 'personal strength', 'civil power', 'personal responsibility' or simply 'taking part'. With the emergence of affective citizenship, the focus shifts onto one's own responsibility and active solidarity, clearly reflecting the trend towards individualization. Solidarity is simply a personal mission and responsibility, and it becomes less and less the duty of the government to organize this solidarity structurally (between generations, between the healthy and the sick, between the employed and unemployed, between the rich and the poor, et cetera).

With the term *individual responsibility* rulers are already searching for a new balance between government and citizens. From a political point of view, the notion of *responsibility* is presented as a solution to both the crisis of the welfare state and the blurring of norms and values.[5] Active

5   Cok Vrooman et al., 'Responsabele burgers, regisserende overheid', in *Een beroep op de burger, Minder verzorgingsstaat, meer eigen verantwoordelijkheid, Sociaal en Cultureel Rapport 2012*, ed. by Vic Veldheer et al. (Den Haag, 2012), p. 11.

citizenship with a focus on private (individual) responsibility often implies less responsibility for the government. It requires little argumentation to demonstrate that this signification fits well with a neoliberal conception of society that represents a receding, minimal state.

FUNCTIONAL CITIZENSHIP

The ever-louder call for personal responsibility reflected a shift from a humanistic view of citizenship towards a functionalist perspective. It is not the whole person that is taken as the subject of civic rights, but the person who can do something, and particularly one who *has* to do something. Only when a person can prove that they fulfil certain functions, or at least intends to fulfil these functions, are they entitled to citizenship. The appeal to active citizenship is therefore often accompanied by an appeal to *obligations*. Someone wishing to be a citizen must therefore show that they want to integrate, to participate, to learn the language, but also that they are available (and flexible) for work. Within the new rhetoric, citizens can only claim civil rights when they perform a function for society, the economy, and the GNP. If they cannot find work, the citizens must volunteer to make their services available to society.

In line with this shift from a humanistic perspective to a functional one, attitudes about government responsibilities have also changed. At least the government's obligations are attached to the notice of civic duties. For example, in the autumn of 2015, a political debate erupted in Belgium on whether to unconditionally grant child benefits without this being linked to school attendance. Can we coerce parents to teach their children in exchange for child benefits?

The Belgian dispute is an example that shows how welfare benefits such as social security, pension schemes, (free) education, etc. are increasingly questioned. What was guaranteed in the Rhineland model as obvious public services for all citizens is not just being reduced. The remaining public services are simultaneously linked to the growing obligations of citizens. These citizens should not only take individual responsibility, but also carry their own risks. The recent transition from scholarships to student loans in the Netherlands, for instance, reduces education as a civil right and collective public duty to a personal choice on one's own account. The same can be said about encouraging private pension savings and private health insurance in several European countries. The dismantling of the welfare state also generates a 'shrinking' of citizenship or, rather, of civil rights. Or, as one phrase doing the rounds has it: the citizen is stripped.

Nearly everywhere, formal or legal citizenship has been reduced to some version of a minimum package. At the same time, this 'minimum citizen' is presented with a wide range of tasks. They must develop their own talents, they must be dynamic, they must integrate socially or simply do good deeds. On the other hand, there is the call to be courageous, to pose political questions, or to adopt a democratic role, a role that is far less reflected in the discourse on citizenship today. Thus, structural and macro-political problems are kept out of sight.

The *active citizen*, according to Biesta, is therefore primarily 'the citizen who will contribute to the reproduction of the existing political order'.[6] Integration and citizenship are cultivated, in his terms, mainly as a matter of socialization. That is to say that civic and integration strategies are designed to introduce individuals to an existing social order and culture without empowering competencies that allow them to question this order.

Criticism and political action, on the other hand, assume processes of subjectification when individuals are confronted with others and others' opinions and learn to argue. Furthermore, they learn to unravel deeper social, political, and economic relations. *Active citizenship*, by contrast, seems to displace the possibility of *critical citizenship*. Already, social criticism oftentimes derives from self-criticism. What goes wrong in the world has to do primarily with one's own limited activity and responsibility. The active citizen is thus encouraged to contribute, but hardly to emancipate. Empowerment nowadays is referred to as primarily a 'social skill' to allow citizens to speak with neighbours and potential employers. Inciting neighbours or colleagues to activism or civil disobedience is not so much part of active citizenship.

6   Biesta, 2011 (see note 2), p. 43.

New conceptions of citizenship fit a democracy of consensus. This assumes a consensus about the existing political model, but also that the decisions based upon and the beliefs about (liberal representative) democracy are consensual. The model thus also assumes that every potential citizen endorses the prevailing norms and values. Those who do not simply fall outside the political space. As the consensus model claims to be correct in assuming that liberal representative democracy is the only true form of politics, anyone who does not endorse this is outlawed. Those who do not want to embrace these values are not excluded for political reasons but on moral grounds. Remember the war rhetoric used by George W. Bush when talking about the 'axis of evil' after the September 11 attacks, remember abusive words such as 'racailles' or 'achterlijke gladiolen' that leading European politicians chose to use after violent outbursts of private citizens. Apparently, the retarded or those who are 'of the devil' never deserve political rights.

The previously identified transition from formal to moral citizenship is thus in line with the shift from a democratic to a moral discourse in the political arena. The fact that democracy, and especially its shape, must constantly be a topic of discussion, as well as the need for dissent among citizens seems to be replaced by the rhetoric of active citizenship and participatory society. But agony and dissent are the core of (deliberative) democracy. *Dissensus* does not just mean discussion, argument, or disagreement between different opinions. Its main concern is to make visible what is not yet visible, to use the words of the French philosopher Jacques Rancière.[7] Dissensus means, for example, to point out civil rights to those who cannot see them under the prevailing policy (or those who don't want to see them) or to those whom the government would not consider entitled to these rights. Dissensus can also mean that the inhabitants of a city may claim certain ecological, social, political or economic rights; rights which no one—apart from themselves—would assume to be allowed to claim. Dissensus questions and breaks the consensus over and over again to always indicate different possibilities.

THE CITIZENS' PARADE
A remarkably positive effect of the outlined evolution is that dissent is mentioned more often. Between governments and markets, between unions and employers, further civil space is opening up worldwide. Perhaps the Indignados and Occupy brought the global vigour of this civil movement most prominently to light. Today, however, processions of activists and citizens' initiatives are holding a parade across the globe. In many cases they operate locally, but their activities apparently are so contagious that they are mirrored all over the world. Virtual networks and social media not only disseminate their messages instantly, also their tactics and organizational forms have a direct global resonance.

7   See Jacques Rancière, *Dissensus: On Politics and Aesthetics* (New York, 2015).

Anyone browsing the web understands quickly that the Internet today is an instruction manual for citizens' initiatives. Be it a subversive or a revolutionary practice, for fun or reformist activities—new means of communication provide these initiatives an immediate global forum. From the Zapatistas in Latin America to Pussy Riot in Russia, from Recetas Urbanas and Sanidad Universal in Spain to the occupation of the Maagdenhuis in Amsterdam, from Anonymous in Canada to Culture 2 Commons and Independent Culture in Croatia, from Teatro Valle Occupato in Italy to Hart boven Hard in Belgium—however diverse the background of all these initiatives may be, they are all kneaded into a new civil society. It has to be said that their actions often disappear as fast as they pop up. But perhaps it is the continuous sequence of activities that counts. Moreover, because of their growing global interconnection they learn from and strengthen one another.

In his book *Networks of Outrage and Hope: Social Movements in the Internet Age*, the Spanish sociologist Manuel Castells explains in depth how, for example, the Egyptian revolution connects with the Kitchenware revolt in Iceland. The flow seems to be unstoppable. However heterogeneous these actions and initiatives may seem, the components for a new civil society are being placed all over the world. Virtual connections and global networks ensure that national governments have less and less control over this phenomenon.

The new civil space that is under construction has a global scope, and the new civilian will be a global citizen. This may all sound somewhat premature, and optimistic, but while the national governments of Europe think that they can restrain their subjects by means of liberal representative democracy, it is hard to deny that a new democracy is in the making in their own backyard. After all, democracy, as is demonstrated in quite a few nations, in fact appears to fulfil a neoliberal agenda. A balanced budget serves as an excuse for further reducing welfare and solidarity structures. If there is anything positive about the ongoing crisis, it is that it is becoming increasingly difficult to hide the true face of the current politics.

MEANING

Liberal representative democracy does not serve civil rights so much, but rather private property and capital. Our election system hides a political-economic ideology. Emerging global social movements and citizen actions are bringing precisely this to light. No matter how varied and volatile the activities of these civic parades may be, the subsequent actions breach the democracy of consensus and models of 'natural' competition each time. Harsh repressive politics of liberal economic measures, cuts and restructuring operations, along with technocratic audits, accreditations, and monitoring administration seem almost heartless. Authorities, administrators or politicians in general are therefore losing public support, as management policy deprives citizenship of all meaning.

A technocratic policy that only navigates according to economic parameters, hinders the granting of meaning. An accumulating bureaucracy crushes any meaning or professional satisfaction that might have been found in education, justice, and health, as much as the economization of (active) citizenship causes a questioning of the very meaning of it all. 'Why am I still doing this?', the teacher asks himself in the evening when he is going through forms on competences and contact hours. 'What is the meaning of all this?', wonders the surgeon when he checks off his operations rate. 'Where is the pleasure in my profession?', muses the judge who now finds himself in a competitive atmosphere with his colleagues. 'And why do they even involve us when we hardly enjoy our civil rights?', the mob thinks when they smash shop windows and street furniture to smithereens.

Both professionalism and citizenship have a great deal to do with meaning. They make it possible to give meaning to our own being, our place and identity in a society. The continuing repressive liberal policy that focuses on quantity now blocks precisely this process of signification. We might put it this way: While workers' revolts and industrial actions were the symptoms of an underlying disease (namely the exploitation of the proletariat in early capitalist times), it is now rather the deprivation of meaning that leads the so-called precariat to despair in the late-capitalist era.

For now, the doctor, teacher, or judge live their life, not yet in poverty; but newcomers may often be given a very modest income. Besides money, there is something else that makes a civilian life. People are finding it increasingly difficult to give meaning to their work within the society in which they dwell. As is well known, this results in stress, burnouts, and sometimes depression. And while refugees and other newcomers find it increasingly difficult to assign themselves meaning in their country of destination, native citizens too are increasingly losing a sense of their national culture and political identity.

When the state is phasing out structural solidarity, hampering free education and health care, the citizens indeed wonder why they still pay taxes. Anyone who is 'quantified' will start calculating more themselves. In short, quantified citizens see themselves more and more in a contractual relationship with society. This rationalized relationship between citizen and state, but also between employee and employer seems simple and functional. What it cannot provide is a 'soul'. Thus the citizen is increasingly deprived of the possibility of a meaningful existence. It is therefore not surprising that the growing group in question comes to rely more and more on violence when faced with the ever-expanding control of a simultaneously shrinking welfare state.

This so-called senseless violence is indeed meaningless in the sense that it is the last straw for many who still demand any sense. When every access to meaning is denied, the fist feels like the last resort to those wishing to be noted, wishing to be provided with significance. And indeed, when the riots do break out, politicians and media suddenly turn their attention to those who have been ignored for decades, who they have neglected in every (electoral) meaning, from whom they have taken away any sense. In short, violence is the final resort of expression for those who are denied all other means of expression. Aggression in the streets, but also towards oneself (as in suicide) is found, in other words, on the edge of culture. When a culture can no longer provide sufficient signs or sense with which to signify a person and his environment, when people have been cut off from culture, sometimes violence seems the only way to reclaim meaning, to write oneself into a culture.[8] That is the paradoxical sense of the 'meaningless' frenzy of the 'racailles' and 'gladiolen'.

THE CULTURAL COMMONS

In contrast to the senseless violence, however, a vitalistic flood of initiatives is emerging to return meaning to work, to citizenship, or simply to life itself. When the mainstream media find it ever more difficult to give a hearing to all voices, when even public broadcasters fail to present a picture of the full cultural richness and diversity in their own lives, and when liberal representative democracy finds it increasingly difficult to tolerate its citizens, then a colourful parade

8   See Pascal Gielen and Thijs Lijster, 'Culture: The Substructure for a European Common', in *No Culture, No Europe: On the Foundation of Politics*, ed. Pascal Gielen (Amsterdam, 2015), pp. 19-66.

of immigrants, artists, scientists, homosexuals, environmentalists, feminists, and trade union activists emerges. What is striking here is that this motley crowd is constantly mixing with each other. New social movements are not only fighting for labour rights in their own lives, as the trade unions of yesteryear once did. Anyone who looks at the bullet points of Indignados or Hart boven Hard will encounter a whole jumble of demands and concerns.

While quite a few mainstream media and politicians easily dismiss them as people who do not know what they want, this is, however, precisely the crux of the matter. The *citizens' parade* represents a total change that can only lay out heterogeneous demands. The point is that ecologists and trade unionists, migrants' and women's rights organizations, artists and doctors, architects and educators are increasingly finding it easier to join in a common struggle. But what is the shared point?

Presumably this is the already identified matter of *meaning*. The *citizens' parade* wants to regain meaning for their existence, their profession, their own being in society. Therefore, the heterogeneous struggle is not exclusively economic, environmental, or political but *cultural*. The actions of Anonymous, Pussy Riot or Recetas Urbanas undeniably have aims that are social, political, or economic, or concern gender equality. But their primary intention is that economics, politics, and society are shaped in a new, different way to permit them to give meaning to themselves and society.

The construction of *meaning* is the central concern of all these movements. Hence culture as a reservoir of meaning and purpose plays a crucial role in their actions. The subversive performances of Pussy Riot, the guerrilla architecture of Recetas Urbanas, and the giants of the Hart boven Hard parade all have in common that they offer an imaginary space in which to conceptualize the world differently. However fictional or utopian they may appear, they do however generate each of these possibilities and, above all, they hold together a motley crowd with the most heterogeneous demands. Precisely this makes *artistic expression* possible. They generate an imaginary space in which the most diverse wishes and desires can be projected.

The growing citizens' actions are no longer limited to such unequivocal concerns as a fair income, global warming or discrimination against women, but are turning more and more to the very *arrangement of our life* in its totality, for which all these things form the constituent components. The purpose of the community of this murmuring crowd is, as stated, to give meaning. And the social place they are trying to generate is called the *commons*.

Between market and government, private and public property, the civilian parade with its public actions, shared city gardens, semi-legal constructions, Wikipedia, open source and creative commons, is restoring a common autonomous place in the city or on the Web. When job satisfaction is managed away, professional enjoyment and pride are downsized, and civil rights are calculated away in a civil budget, the commons provide one of the few remaining sanctuaries for meaning.

We should not delude ourselves: the common is not a harmonious community. There is no hippie romanticism here, but a lot of squabbling and bickering set the scene of the commons. Naturally, conflicting demands and desires collide in the battle for meaning and purpose. But it is precisely this dissensus that keeps a truly democratic culture alive. And we should be quite optimistic about this. The more rulers hide behind budget deficits, the higher management stacks bureaucracy, and the more civil rights we lose, the bigger the hunger for meaning and culture will become and the harder the commons will act. Sometimes it happens through violent outbursts, but more and more colourful and meaningful parades are being held too. The citizens' parade is spreading worldwide to help bury neoliberalism once and for all, to give life meaning again.

This text was first published in Defne Ayas et al., eds., *How to Gather: Acting Relations, Mapping Positions* (Moscow, 2017), pp. 405–418.

Pascal Gielen

The Global Civil Parade

THE CRISIS OF THE SOCIAL IMAGINARY AND BEYOND

Bojana Cvejić and Ana Vujanović

II – COMMUNITIES AND DEMOCRACY

The last and least discussed crisis we recognize today, after the crisis of democracy, the financial crisis, the environmental crisis, the crisis in education, and so on, is the crisis of the social imaginary. Perhaps the social imaginary doesn't appear to be at all in decline in public debates, because we haven't been aware of having (or losing) it.

But instead of being fatally pessimistic, we might do better to remember the times when society and the imagination were not deficient and incompatible categories, and to describe what it is that is missing and what prevents us today from investing beliefs and images in a social idea. Those times are historical, and are linked to societies that have undergone socialism and social democracy in the twentieth century.

Or we could be more reserved about that past. If the main question here is 'Why is it so difficult or why does it seem utopian to think of a society that is not neoliberal-capitalist?' we cannot but think of the real socialism of the twentieth century as the recent real existing alternative to capitalism, which also proved to be problematic because it caused as many problems as it tried to resolve.

Let's begin with the first lines of Roberto Esposito's book *Communitas*:

Nothing seems more appropriate today than thinking community; nothing more necessary, demanded, and heralded by a situation that joins in a unique epochal knot the failure of all communisms with the misery of new individualisms.[1]

This claim implies that the failure of real socialism: a) compromises communism as an alternative social order; b) weakens the current left-wing political options in capitalist society, and c) calls all alternatives into question in advance, since the previous alternative, i.e., socialism, failed, despite being big, strong, and supported by states.

These are serious limitations to the social imaginary today. But what about the misery of the new individualism? We need to imagine social configurations that are capable of responding to it without repeating the recipes for and mistakes of real socialism. We simply must do so to get out of the deadlock, the 'unique epochal knot' of which Esposito warns us.

We could probably begin by defining the temporal problem first: imagination is invested in a future. But 'There is no future' is the bitter message of all neoliberal reforms today that undercut the horizon of the welfare state, and the refrain of

1   Roberto Esposito, *Communitas: The Origin and Destiny of Community* (Stanford, 2010), p. 1.

many protests against global capitalism (from students to environmentalists). Could we say that 'no future' as a social mood grows against the background of presentism, a conception and an experience of time in which only the present is 'real'? Definitely! History is revised in ways that treat the memory of past times as an obstacle to contemporaneity and progress (think of the revision of communism and socialism after 1989, or the reductions in elementary educational curricula in subjects that are deemed less useful, such as history or philosophy). Presentism prevails in current capitalism, which operates with volatility and flexibility in 'the instant', against the ticking clock of finance. The unit of measurement for lived and experienced time, the instant, seems ever shorter given the apparent pace of social acceleration.

It seems that if the present is to pass favourably, it must hijack the near future; that is, predict it and control it moment by moment. Long-term projections into the distant future—plans like the notorious five-year plans for economic development, or just slowly and gradually planning one's education according to sheer affinities, not career prospects—are discouraged. Work contracts are currently reaching maximum degrees of temporariness, relieving the employer of many social obligations towards the employee in the future.

This paralyzes the capacity to imagine the future. Moreover, it spreads the fear of 'no future', marking uncertainty with a negative prefix. It puts the subject in a waiting-lurking mode, listening to the tendencies of the present as imminent threats or unexpected opportunities in order to manage a short-term future.

Another topic: long ago, Hannah Arendt wrote about 'the common world' as a premise and prospect of politics, at least in a democratic society.[2] Today this is considered a problematic, oppressively unitary and reductive notion. Nevertheless, we would like to raise the provocative question: Could the crisis of social imaginary be a result of the loss of the common world?

Not so long ago, in the French daily *Le Monde*, Alain Badiou argued that 'we live in one world'.[3] Unfortunately, this maxim is relegated to only one common concern we must share: the planet, and its likely demise in the 'anthropocene', for which we are partly responsible. All other causes are considered too partisan to mobilize for collectively, and dismissed as the fragmentary demands of different parts/parties of the multitude defending their lost benefits. Another obstacle to

2   Hannah Arendt, *The Human Condition* (Chicago, 1958).
3   Alain Badiou, 'Le courage du présent', *Le Monde*, 13 February 2010.

the social imaginary is therefore that the ideal of the social totality has been eclipsed. Society cannot be envisaged anymore due to a perspectival logic that constantly divides, repartitions, and miscounts the population according to new fault lines, identities and communities, rights to citizenship, benefits, privileges and expulsions. This tireless fragmentation has penetrated the very language in which subjects express themselves in the first person, carefully guarded by emphatic appositions ('for my part', 'in my view', 'as far as I'm concerned'). The tolerance of difference becomes repressive when the function of saying 'we' in the context of a social vision has been debilitated.

The situation now is intriguing. There is fragmentation and specification of concerns and interests, and at the same time—besides the two problems we mentioned above—we quite often come across the problem of great expectations that should correspond to great dissatisfaction. Think of the protests in Madrid, Athens, and elsewhere. Or let's speak about art for a moment. The general crisis of social imagination is also manifested in art. Let's consider, for instance, the contemporary performing arts scenes in Europe. We often see brilliant critiques of neoliberal and individualist capitalism, but only rarely are other possibilities affirmed. This failure is not inexplicable. On the one hand, as has been extensively discussed, neoliberal capitalism is highly flexible and it is possible to become complicit with it even while one is aware of its detrimental effects on the global scale. That might explain why cynicism in art, among other places, is somewhat popular today—cynically recognizing a disagreeable state of affairs without engaging with a critical or constructive stance from which to change it. It's cool to be cynical, because it shows that you are smart, capable of navigating the 'system', and in that way superior to the others who are blindly overlooking the dark sides of the 'system' that they are part of. The other possible problem associated with the crisis of social imagination we see here is that artists often have (too many) doubts about what to affirm, since it looks as though everyone is expecting some big 'something', and that may indeed paralyze the imagination. Somehow there has been no satisfactory idea for some time, nothing 'strong' to stand up for. This is evident from the very vocabulary of contemporary art, where everything is just a provisional proposal...

There is more than one difference at play: for example, the difference between specific concerns and fragmentary special interests on the one hand, and the grand narratives of social visions on the other. The obstacle to social imagination is a lack of systemic thought in which the multiplicity of demands requires thorough rethinking and a restructuring of production and distribution, citizenship, and the public sphere; in a word, a social revolution. But revolution is probably the least popular dream one can have today, censored as it is by the cynically enlightened consciousness ('We know better...', 'Everybody knows it is doomed to fail'). Indeed, what is the horizon of the social imaginary once the option of social revolution has been removed from it?

Isn't it also a problem of ideology, or of its absence? From the historical perspective of the Cold War, ideology provided the ideas with which society was necessarily imagined and defended. Once ideology had been ruled out and was overcome by the victory of a liberal democracy based on capitalism, an ideological vacuum based on the 'value of the immanence of life' was installed.

The sense of an ideological vacuum has become starkly evident in the wake of Daesh, or more precisely when we compare it to the allure of the Daesh ideology, which has recruited youth from the prosperous Western democracies. The goal of living one's own life in Western societies is not evil or morally

146

wrong, but it is politically and socially problematic when the desires and needs of this individual life are privatized, become detached from the social totality and exist in competition with those of other private individuals. The problem lies in the inability to recognize that the pre-individual heritage (language, habits, sensations, history) and the transindividual horizon (the capacity to produce together) form the generic base on which the individual can prosper. Social consciousness of the pre-individual and transindividual enriches the generic base, in which there is more abundance and multiplicity to share and distribute among the many than the image of scarcity and austerity might suggest to individuals who must struggle to obtain their share.

Why should this plea for social consciousness sound obsolete and odd? This may be related to one more problem we would like to mention here. Digitality—besides the many innovations it has brought to the areas of information, communication, transport, and the flow of money—means that numbers trump ideas. Predictive analytics by way of algorithms has not only become central to the digital economy and speculative financial markets; it has also penetrated the domain of social reason. Thus algorithms are developed to measure social activity and interaction. Computational logic is applied wherever it can increase financial profit. It brags about being able to make correlations between facts that can predict and control the future in ways that suggest science fiction. Current sociological debates have addressed the question of whether the logic that explains social phenomena will be replaced by the logic of correlation, which means mapping correspondences among heterogeneous data. The punchline of the argument from predictive analytics is: 'Numbers speak for themselves.' In a society in which decision-making primarily relies on numbers and concomitant procedures, ideas are a thing of the past, as are concerns and substantive arguments; they are outdated and mistrusted.

While we have mainly outlined the negative aspects of the crisis of social imagination, we would now like to affirm the elements and traces of emergent social imaginaries, those that we may still see develop on a larger scale in Europe and beyond. In general, we consider art a perfect place for imagining the social and for social imagination. This is our biggest example of constantly emergent social imaginaries, so to speak. At bottom, in art, every single work or project has a potential to project one possible world. We need not expect these worlds to be large, complete, spectacular, intellectually elaborated, and so on. As they are, that is, as small, chaotic, clumsy, experimental, affective, and so on, they probably cannot change society like a social revolution, coup d'état, and so on could. But they can still hack the virtual world of our society rather than 'leaving it alone' in its actuality. That is why the fact that contemporary art is so reserved, so doubtful, worries us.

With such expectations of art, we could project an additional criterion for the evaluation of art, apart from the conceptual. If every work of art must nowadays implicitly answer the question 'What is art?' (i.e., what it proposes as the concept of art), then an image of society can be derived indirectly from that same work of art. This is not just a matter of acknowledging the political aspect of every artwork. It also means that we must make an effort of the imagination as viewers of art; must think or imagine what kind of society this artwork recommends, how it conceives of its social and aesthetic ideals, how it organizes itself structurally, what its modes of perception and action, its actors and its beneficiaries are. This could be a test for every artwork, a mental exercise: what would society be like *after* this work of art?

Speaking of the politico-economic sphere, one concrete trace of an emergent social imaginary is to be found in the debate on the universal and unconditional basic income, also referred to as the social or living wage. While the idea of the social wage was introduced in the 2000s by the Italian post-workerist theorists Antonio Negri and Paolo Virno, it is now promoted by the techno-utopian Silicon Valley 'workers' and has reached governments in the UK and the Netherlands, while in Finland they are testing it on a limited scale. One of the advantages of this measure, as conceived by the biopolitical thinkers, is that the social wage will diminish competition and increase solidarity among citizens, leaving them more time to engage with society. However, these governments are wagering on diminishing misery, yet only by keeping the existing economic system in check. A more radical transformation of capitalism would be required to address the real gaps that impede social equality between the wealthy and the poor.

Finally, we would like to mention another, much broader element of the social imaginary today: the social solidarity movement among citizens in Athens. After their experience of organizing a parallel society on Syntagma Square, the Greek citizens have continued to self-organize in the domains of public service in which the state faltered (medical help, education, art and culture, hosting refugees). They explicitly disentangle themselves from the political parties, claiming that they come together on a purely social, civic basis, the sharing of resources through generosity, or even just because 'they are social'. At the same time, the French people were protesting against their putatively socialist President in a movement which, much like the early Podemos in Spain, gathered young citizens to assemble and discuss in the main city square. They chose to meet in the dark hours, in a deliberate inversion of appearing in public by day—Nuit Debout (Night Awake, or Night Standing Up).[4] As with the previous social movements in 2011 and later, it remains to be seen whether and how the social imagination can be renewed wholesale beyond a small percentage of sympathetic citizens and activists.

This text is a slightly revised version of a text published under the same title in Marie Nerland ed., *The Imaginary Reader* (Bergen, 2016), pp. 34-37.

4   As a friend-participant told us, 'nuit debout' was originally a play on the concept of 'nuit blanche', the evenings when all the museums are open. Their idea was that having protests and concerts in the evening could change the tone of the gathering, as experienced in the daytime protests that many found monotonous. It wasn't expected at that time that 'nuit debout' would become the name of the occupation of the Place de la République.

Bojana Cvejić and Ana Vujanović

The Crisis of the Social Imaginary and Beyond

HOW TO CHANGE THE WORLD
Lia Perjovschi

II — COMMUNITIES AND DEMOCRACY

These diagrams are part of a Contemporary Art Archive (CAA) Kit, in which they function as recuperative tools that contribute to the creation of both local and transnational communities.

COLLECTIVES.
CREATIVES.
THINKERS.
VISIONARIES.
COMMUNITIES.
ARTISTS

INSPIRING EXAMPLES OF FRESH
THINKING AND PRACTICES
THAT TRY TO CONNECT.
AND INTEGRATE WHAT
SEEMS TO BE (FALLING APART)

TO REIMAGINE ANOTHER FUTURE

THE REIMAGINING WORLD

DREAM
SHARING
INVENTING

(RE)-THINKING
DOING
CHANGING

COURAGE
SPACE
PERSEVERANCE

AS A CULTURAL
CHANGE-MAKING
POSITIVE
VISION
ACTION

CULTURE

DEMOCRACY

COURAGEOUS
CITIZENS

HOW CULTURE
GENERATES
CHANGE

THE 10TH ANNIVERSARY
OF THE ECF
PRINCESS MARGRIET AWARD
FOR CULTURE

THE BOOK
2017.

PMA —
AN ANNUAL AWARD
(ACKNOWLEDGING) AND (AMPLIFYING)
THE WORK OF.
INDIVIDUALS AND
COLLECTIVES WHOSE
CREATIVE WORK CAN
TRULY MAKE A
DIFFERENCE IN
EUROPE'S SOCIETIES

THE EUROPEAN
CULTURAL
FOUNDATION

COMMUNITY

CENTRE OF PLEASE

AN INDEPENDENT AND
(IMPACT DRIVEN)
FOUNDATION THAT
ACCELERATES
CATALYSES CONNECTS AND
COMMUNICATES CIVIL SOCIETY
INITIATIVES (IN ART AND
CULTURE)

GRANTS
PROGRAMMES
EXCHANGES

— AN INDEPENDENT
FOR.
(EUROPE) AS A. —

OPEN
INCLUSIVE
DEMOCRATIC
SPACE.

RAPIDLY SHRINKING
& DEMOCRACY — BELIEF IN A
UNITED EUROPE
— DISTRUST 'BRUSSELS'
— BREXIT
EXCLUSIONARY PRACTICES — ECONOMICALLY
— POLITICALLY
— CULTURALLY MOTIVATED
— CREATED DEEP DIVIDES

FRAGMENTATION & SOLIDARITY
FRAGMENTED AND POLARIZED WORLD
Rising AUTHORITARIANISMS
XENOPHOBIC POPULIST SENTIMENTS
(2 D)
+ THEIR COMMUNITIES ARE EXPLORING
Negative EFFECT ON EU CITIZENS

NEW APPROACHES
TO DECISION-MAKING

ACTIVISM
ENGAGED CITIZENSHIP

CULTURAL CHANGE MAKERS
'MOVERS AND SHAKERS' OF
CULTURAL FIELD
PUTTING GREAT EFFORTS — REINVENTING
INSTITUTIONS
PARTICIPATORY PRACTICES

PROJECT:
A SYSTEM OF GOVERNMENT
BY THE WHOLE POPULATION
OR ALL THE ELIGIBLE MEMBERS
OF A STATE. — THROUGH ELECTED
REPRESENTATIVES
— PARLIAMENTARY DEMOCRACY
— PEOPLE POWER
BUILDING
— ORGANIZING
— DEVELOPMENT
— NETWORKS
FUTURE
STILL TO COME.

OR IMAGE.
WHO HAVE
IN COMMON
NORMS

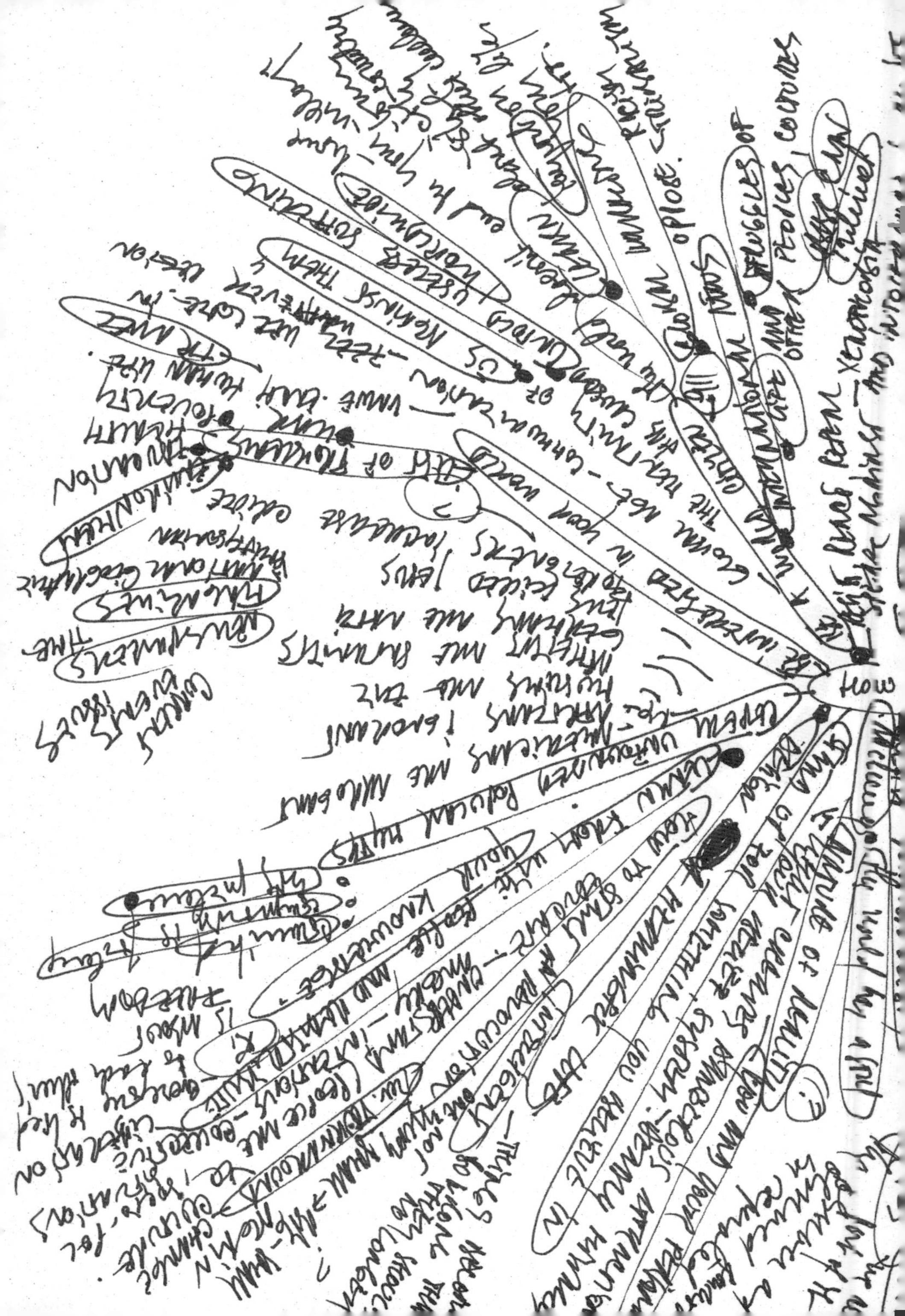

PASS THE BOOK

POWER

KNOWLEDGE AND INSPIRATION — POWER APPLIED

Sources of

RECORD yourself — SPEAK your mind

Leave it in a public space

FEED A NATION

Give a man a fish and you feed him for a day — Teach a man to fish and you feed him for a lifetime.

Culture

Socially engaged citizens

COMMUNICATE — NEVER FEEL POWERLESS as an individual

— Learning about the world today

HELP CHANGE THE WORLD

ABUSE
POVERTY
POLLUTION

DONATE MONEY

VOLUNTEER — to do anything

Local volunteer organisations

RECYCLE

Reduce poverty

Do not travel

BE AN ADVOCATE — Speak up about injustices in the world

How to do this BETTER?

HELP OTHERS

Contribute

Positive

TRUTH

Social Protest

RESOURCES

CONCENTRATE / COMMUNICATE

PREDICTIONS.

FUTURE

?

THE EFFECT OF CLIMATE CHANGE will be INEVITABLE

AUTHORITARIANISM

ROBOTS T...

SMARTER

AUTOMATE

HOLOGRAMS

MIND UPLOADING

ECONOMY.
POLITIC - CHAOS
IS THE
WORLD -

ANGER

POST TRUTH

CYNICISM

POST PRODUCTION

NIHILISM

NARCISSISM -

REQUIRE DESTRUCTIVE ATOMIC-SCALE SCANNING OF THE BRAIN

KILLED. REPLACED BY A DUPLICATE

THE ORIGINAL BRAIN IS DESTROYED REPLACED BY A DIGITAL BEING

NOTY

D WILL BE ROUTINE ?

?

FAVELAS
POOR HOUSING
SMALL UNITS
URBANISED + PEOPLE .
TO BIG
COMPLEX

CRIME
SOCIETY

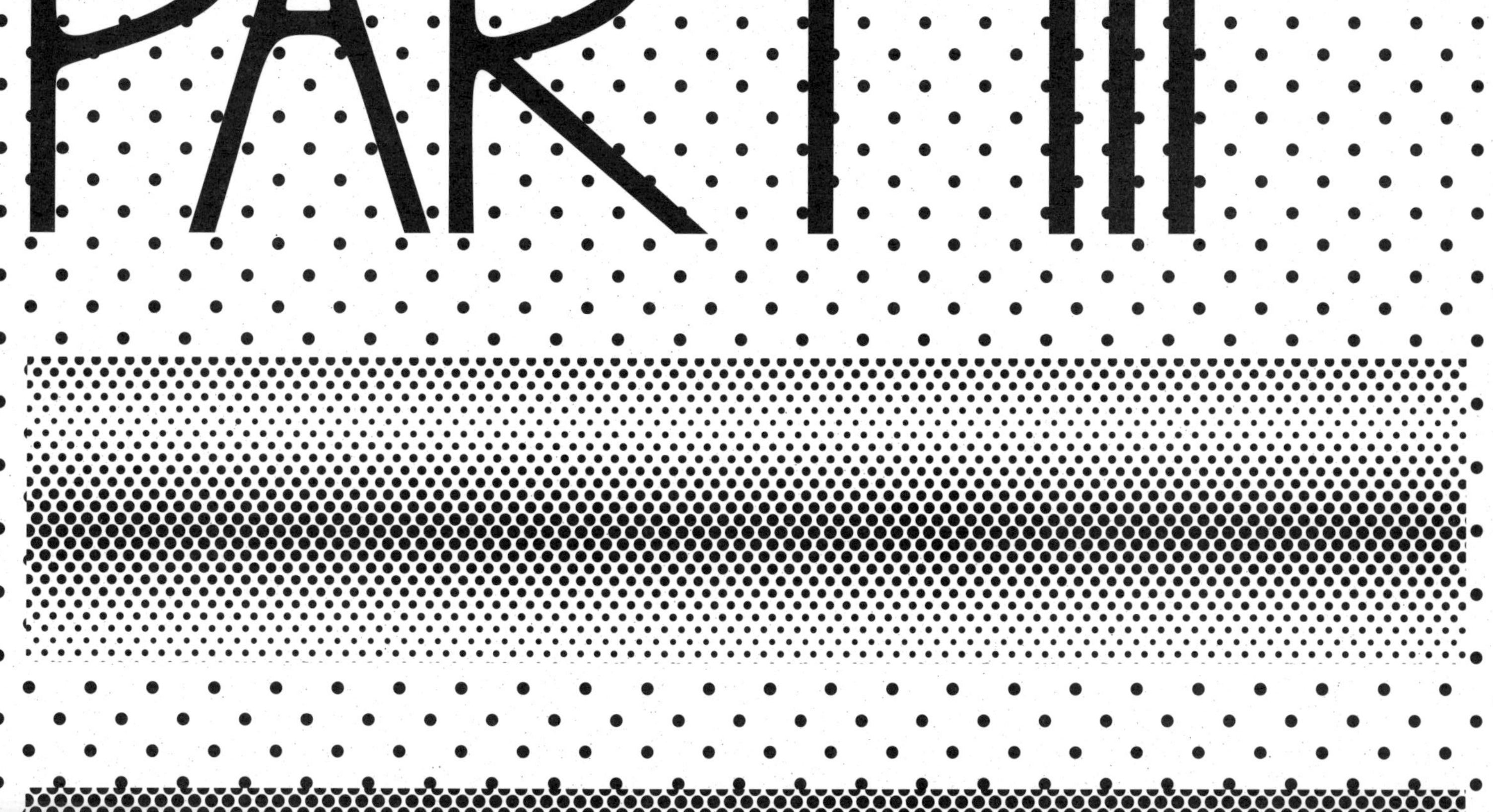

PART III

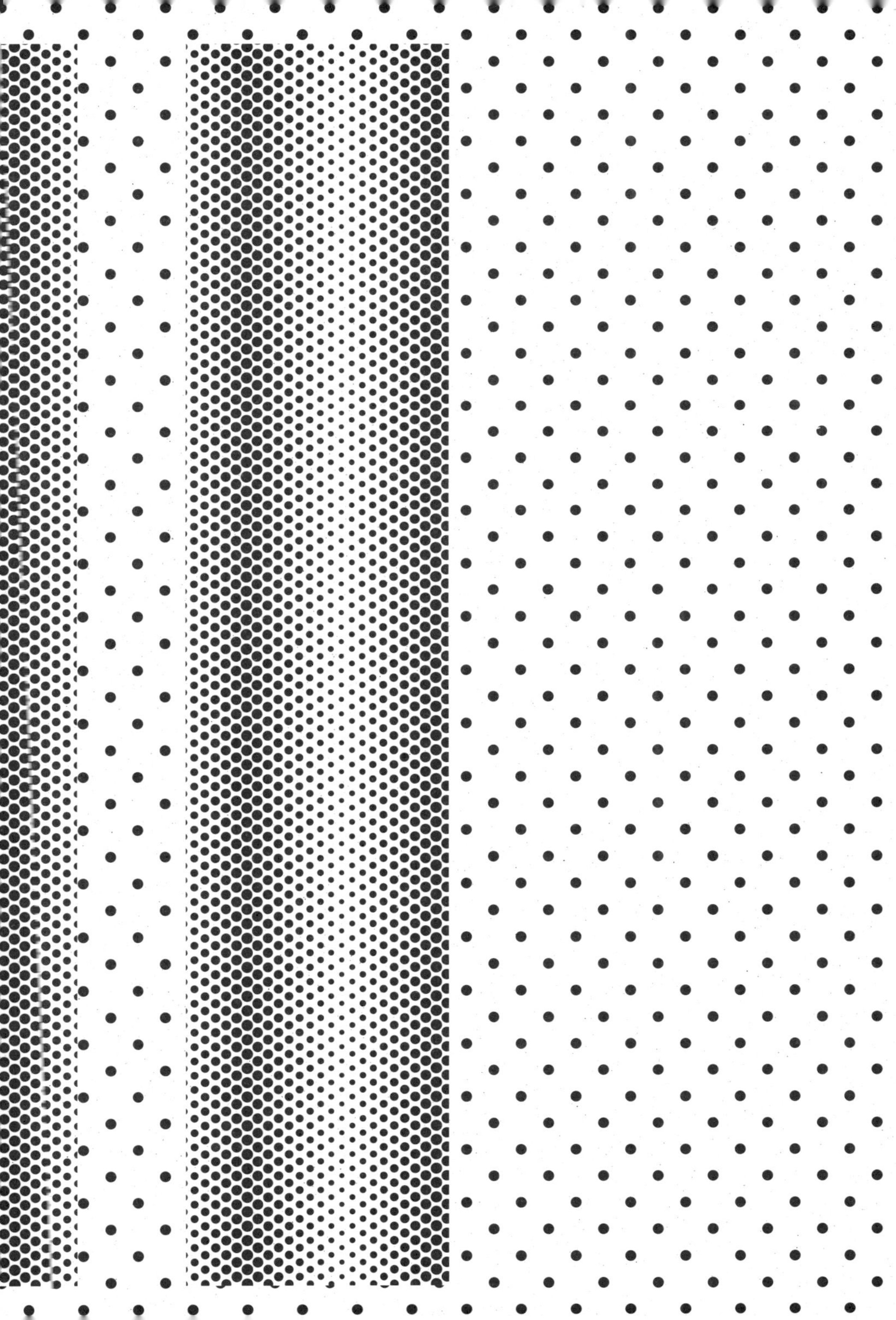

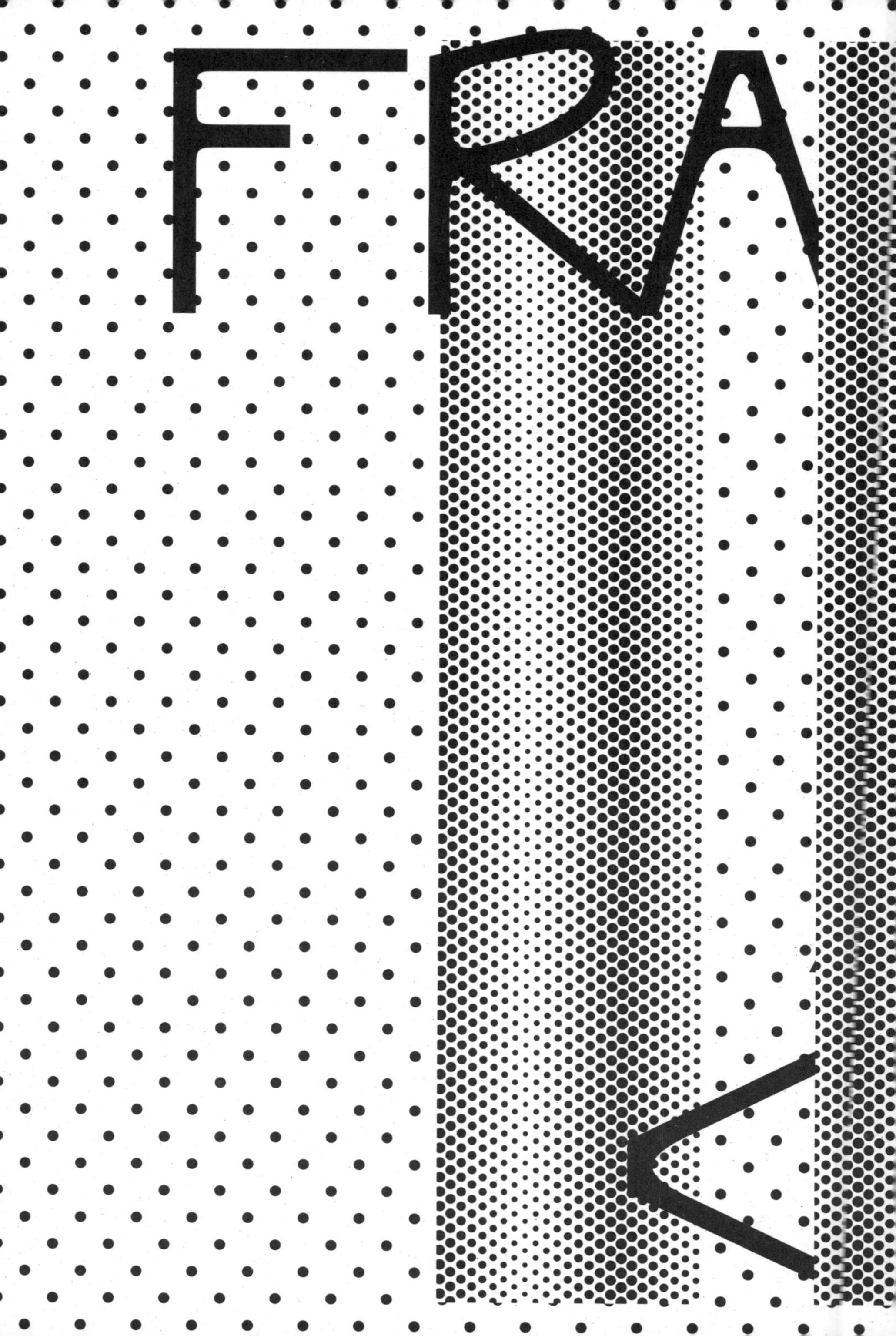

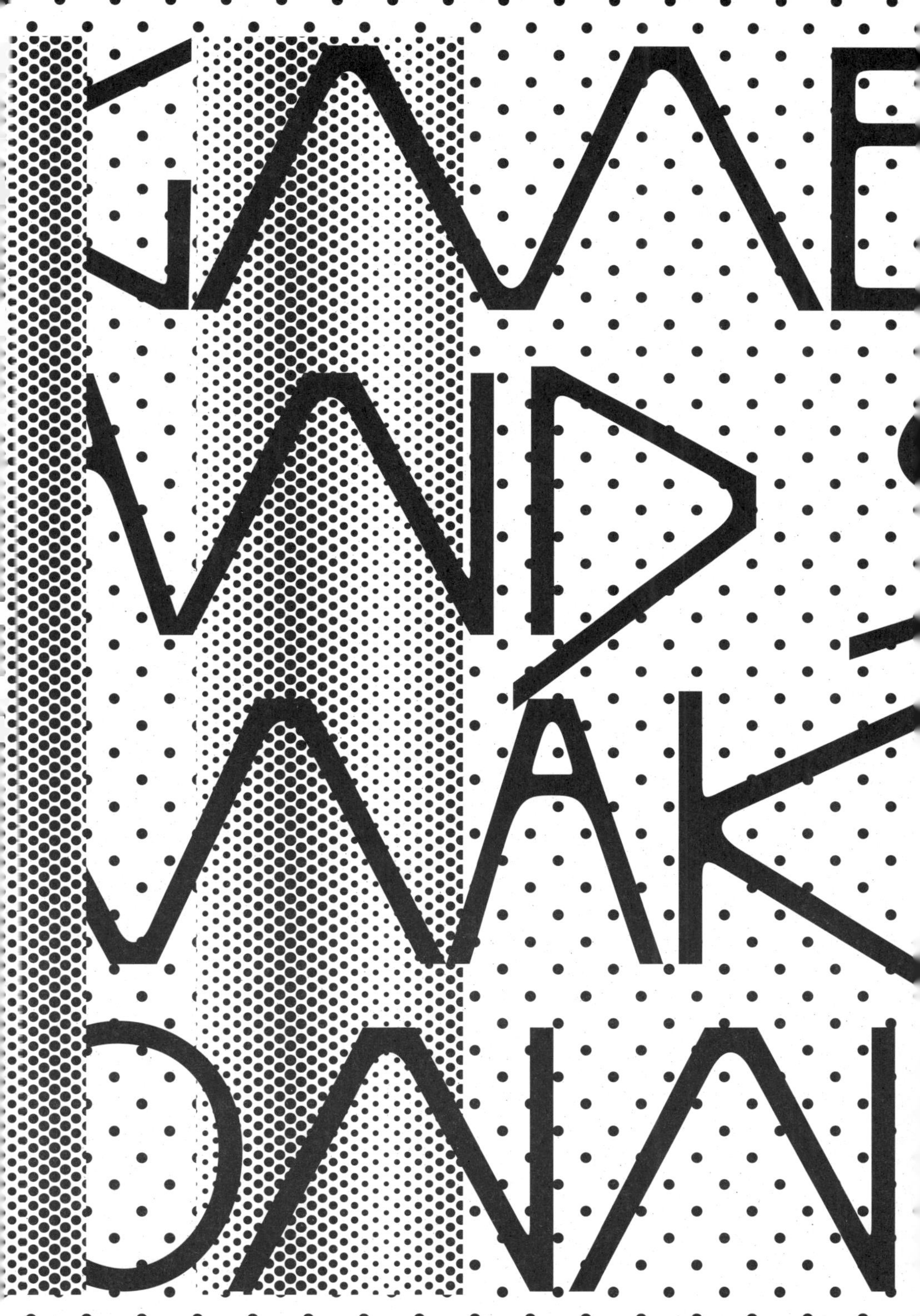

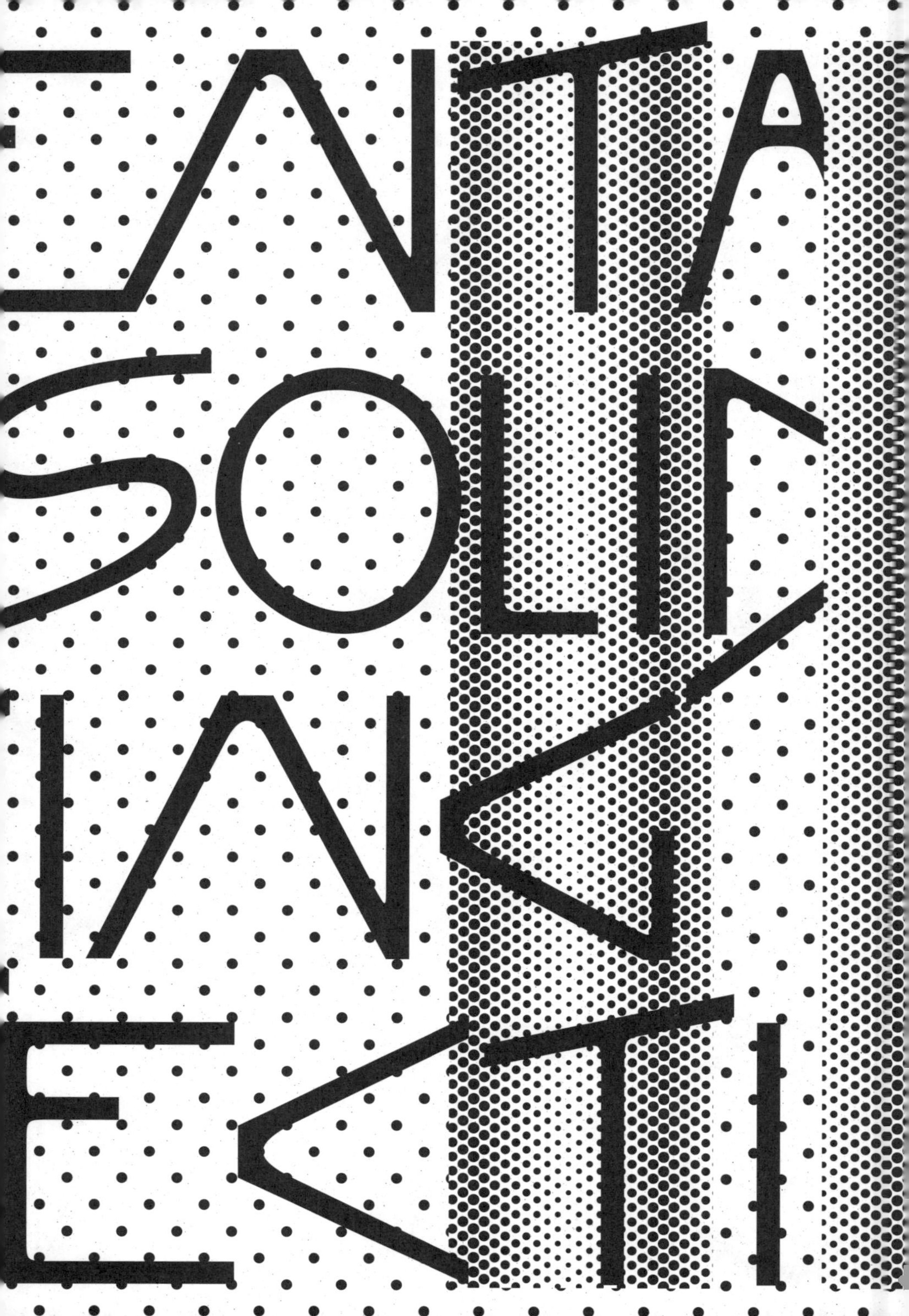

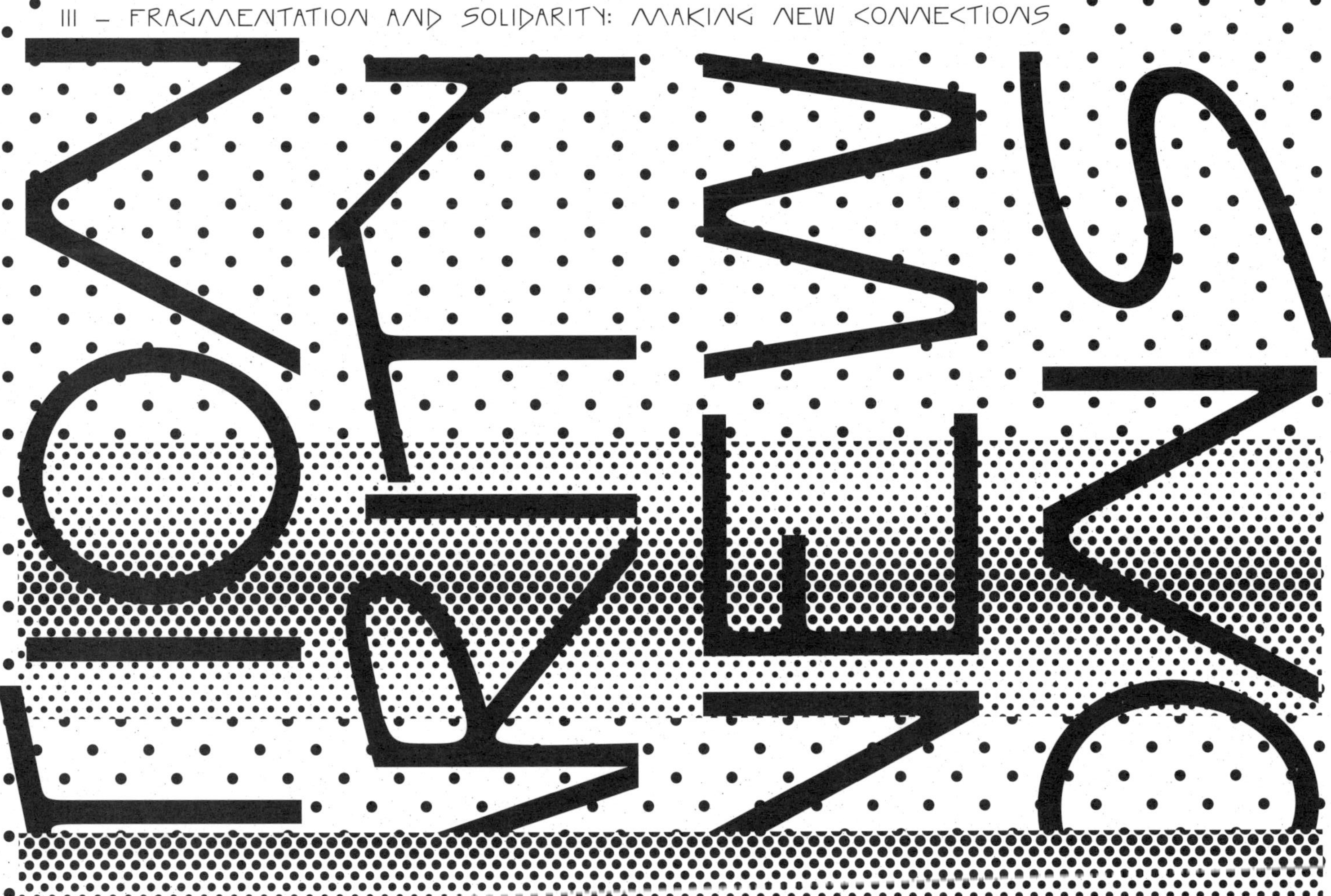
III – FRAGMENTATION AND SOLIDARITY: MAKING NEW CONNECTIONS

III – FRAGMENTATION AND SOLIDARITY

THE LANGUAGE
OF EXPULSION

Saskia Sassen

III — FRAGMENTATION AND SOLIDARITY

When we discuss rising inequality, poverty, imprisonment, foreclosed homes, and other injustices, simply engaging in familiar discussions about these increases in disparities does not capture the larger reality we must face. We need new language. I use the term 'expulsions' to mark the radicalness of that necessary shift.

For instance, we need new language to express the fact that a growing number of adult men in poor neighbourhoods in the United States have not ever held a job; the phrase 'long-term unemployment' is much too vague and fails to capture a radical structural condition. Our language must recognize that the 52 million people identified by the United Nations High Commissioner for Refugees (UNHCR) as 'displaced people' are almost never returning home, because their 'homes' have been replaced by a new luxury building, a plantation, a war zone. Both the long-term unemployed and the long-term displaced have, in fact, been expelled from society.

These, and many other expulsions take on specific forms in each location of the world, and they have specific contents in diverse domains: economy, society, politics. Indeed, they are so specific in each place and domain—and are usually studied in these very specific contexts—that it is difficult to see that they might be the surface manifestations of deeper trends that today cut across the familiar divisions. To return to the two examples mentioned here: experts on long-term unemployment in the Global North do not really study the displaced in the Global South, and vice-versa. And yet, at ground level, these displacements share a simple, common element: There are people being (usually permanently) cast out of what had been their lives.

We must find ways to discuss the systemic edges hidden deep inside the territory of the national. These edges are not to be confused with national borders or other politico-administrative divisions, even though they may coincide in some cases. Further, once the unemployed or the displaced, or so many other versions of the expelled, cross this systemic edge, they become a bit invisible; they are less likely to be counted in measures of GDP per capita or in a census. This is becoming a bit invisible as it applies to people, places, failed small businesses, neighbourhoods destroyed by hurricanes, neighbourhoods destroyed by mortgage foreclosures, and more.

All these expulsions, and so many others not mentioned here, coexist with growth in 'the' economy, even if the space of that economy is shrinking. This coexistence of growth (as conventionally measured) and these expulsions further add to the invisibility of those who are expelled from job and home.

Complex forms of knowledge we admire come into play in many of these expulsions—notably, advanced mathematics for the algorithms of finance and complex legal innovations to enable the massive land-grabs that took off in 2006. I see this mal-deployment of knowledge as a major issue in our current global political economy. It brings to the fore the fact that forms of knowledge and intelligence we respect and admire are often at the origin of long transaction chains that can end in simple brutalities. One example of a simple expulsion would be the low-paid unhealthy jobs that are part of the complex logistics of outsourcing. These complex forms of knowledge produce grand expulsions, as when one builds an enormous dam that buries whole villages and farmlands, thereby making visible its destructive side.

Certain extreme cases make that mal-deployment of knowledge sharply visible. For instance, the so-called subprime mortgage developed in the 2000s was a financial project aimed at developing new types of asset-backed securities and collateralized debt. It is not to be confused with the

state-sponsored, sub-prime mortgages of an earlier
period, aimed at genuinely helping modest-income
families to own a home. The new versions of subprime
mortgages used the modest homes involved to meet
the growing demand for asset-backed securities by
investors, in a market where the outstanding value
of derivatives was $630 trillion, or 14 times the
value of global GDP.

Investors were clamouring for some real
assets backing securities, not just derivatives on
interest rates and so on in long chains of hypothet-
icals. The complexity of financial engineering was
deployed to de-link the actual (modest) value of the
house and of the mortgage from the asset-backed
security aimed at the high-finance circuit. Various
financial manoeuvres were used to camouflage the
modesty of the actual material assets. A high-finance
instrument was developed on the backs of 'the little
people'. The challenge was to delink such that even
if the buyers of the house could not pay, it really did
not matter—the high-investment circuit would have
made its money, and only those who had held on to
the mortgages would suffer with the eventual crisis.

When this short and brutal history was
over in 2010, over 13 million such contracts had
been signed and 9 million households—that could

be about 30 million people or more—had lost their homes, according to the Federal Reserve. Now this instrument is circulating in Europe, where every year several hundred thousand households are losing their homes. Some of the highest numbers of foreclosures in Europe are happening in Germany[1], the country we think of as having avoided all forms of the crisis.

When we consider them all together, the diverse expulsions across countries may well have a greater impact on the shaping of our world than the rapid economic growth in India, China, and a few other countries. Indeed, such expulsions can coexist with economic growth as counted by standard measures.

These expulsions don't simply happen; they are made. The instruments for this 'making' range from elementary policies to complex techniques requiring specialized knowledge and intricate organizational formats. And the channels for expulsion vary greatly. They include austerity policies that have helped shrink the economies of Greece and Spain, and environmental policies that overlook the toxic emissions from enormous mining operations.

Historically, the oppressed have often risen against their 'masters'. Today, despite

1   Saskia Sassen, 'What all is getting expelled…and once expelled is invisible', www.opendemocracy.net/can-europe-make-it/saskia-sassen/what-all-is-getting-expelledand-once-expelled-is-invisible (26 June 2014).

movements of resistance around the globe, such opposition is often prevented by the way in which the oppressed have been expelled and survive at a great distance from their oppressors.

Addressing this reality full on will require recognizing the radical character of these expulsions —a bit more job growth, a bit more help with housing: none of this will be enough to restore a measure of social justice in this world.

This essay is based on Saskia Sassen's book *Expulsions: Brutality and Complexity in the Global Economy* (Cambridge, MA, 2014). It was first published by Truthout.org: www.truth-out.org/opinion/item/25235-the-language-of-expulsionon (30 July 2014).

III – FRAGMENTATION AND SOLIDARITY

Saskia Sassen

The Language of Expulsion

III – FRAGMENTATION AND SOLIDARITY

EUROPEAN OTHERS

Fatima El-Tayeb

III – FRAGMENTATION AND SOLIDARITY

Being European while not being white and Christian does not only put one in a strange place, but also in a strange temporality: Europeans who lack one or both of these qualities tend to be read as having just arrived or even as still being elsewhere—if not physically, then at least culturally. In European discourse (legally, culturally, socially, economically, academically...) the term 'migrant' describes someone who moves across borders, but also includes all racialized European communities, which are reframed as non-European through their ascribed permanent status as migrating (from somewhere that is not Europe). This status is transmitted across generations and thus increasingly decoupled from the actual event of migration, shifting the meaning of 'migrant' from a term indicating movement to one indicating a static, hereditary state. In other words, movement into Europeanness is impossible as long as racialized difference is still visible.

Racialized populations are thus positioned within a spatial and temporal paradox: they are permanently frozen in the moment of arrival —and the further away the actual moment/ movement of migration, the stronger the paradox, i.e. the 'queerness' of their presence in space and time. The current so-called third generation of post-war labour and post-colonial migrants is perceived to be more alien and out of place and time in Europe than their grand-parents, the first generation of actual migrants, exactly because they are (made) impossible as an internal presence within (and by) the ideology of normalized colour-blindness that places 'race' and thus racialized populations necessarily outside of Europe.

While the European Union has been firmly established as a key political and economic player in the post-Cold War world, often appearing as the more humane, balanced alternative to militarized US domination (and as successfully having shed its imperialist past), the question of what exactly Europe is appears more unresolved than ever. Instead, there is an anxiety-ridden debate around threats to a European identity alternately defined as Christian, secular, and Judeo-Christian and, at least implicitly, as white, as if uncertainty about Europe's economic and political future could be ended by expelling those embodying 'non-Europeanness', that is, communities of colour, in particular black, Roma, and Muslim.

At the same time, when working on racism and Europe, one is often faced with the assumption that such prejudice is non-existent on the continent—many white Europeans go as far as to claim that they 'do not understand race', usually when referencing a supposed US American obsession with it. Europeans tend to see the relevance given to race as one of the differences, if not the central difference, between Europe and the United States, and attempts to point to the important role of race (and racism) in European identity formations are frequently framed as enforcing an Americanized 'political correctness' without meaningful European context.

Instead they are framed as an attempt at silencing necessary critiques of migrant communities and their supposed innate sexism, anti-Semitism, and homophobia (the prominence of discourses around 'migrant extremism' notwithstanding, there is an equally prominent assumption that it is taboo to criticize these communities). And indeed, at first glance it might seem as if Europe exists outside of the US American (post) racial temporality. While the latter is built on a narrative of having successfully overcome intolerance and discrimination, the myth of European colour-blindness claims that Europe never was 'racial' (anti-Semitism is still often analyzed as both an exception to this and as clearly separable from racism). That is, despite the origin of the concept of race in Europe and the explicitly race-based policies of both its fascist regimes and its colonial empires, the dominant assumption is that this history had no impact on the continent and its internal structures.

The repression of the long history of race and racism in Europe in turn produces the continent's contemporary 'multicultural' state (associated with visual markers of non-Europeanness, be it dark skin or a headscarf) as a novelty, which requires adjustment in the best case and resistance in the worst, and which, most importantly, can simply be declared to have 'failed'. Multiculturalism in this sense does not merely describe a reality (which cannot be undone at will), but represents a particular discursive means to manage and control this reality through a narrative of linear global advancement that places Europe/ the West as the inevitable hub of progress and human rights. This narrative produces the need and requires the ability to constantly rewrite history in order to re-centre Europe, resulting in the repression of colonial and (state) socialist legacies in the production of hegemonic discourses of history and memory in the contemporary moment.

This spatio-temporal regime of knowledge management configures racialized populations

as displaced and anachronistic: they are perceived as being in transit, coming from elsewhere, momentarily here but without any
roots in their 'host nation'. Centring on the
Enlightenment and the French Revolution
but reaching back to the ancient Greek and
Roman Empires, and forward to include the
less celebratory realities of the Second World
War, fascism, and Stalinism, a linear narrative
of Europeanness has been constructed and
is used as foundation for an identity that transcends national divisions but remains firmly
within internal limits.

Such a narrative requires a clear separation between what is European and what is
not—an impossible task that invariably produces tensions that threaten the coherence
of the construct. Historically, these tensions
have centred on race and religion as markers
of non-Europeanness. The temporal suspen-
sion of racialized communities, as here but
not really belonging, also produces an out-
of-placeness: due to their precarious position
within Europe, communities of colour are
defined through an excess of movement while
simultaneously experiencing an extreme
lack of it. Their discursive framing as eternal
migrants, permanently stuck in a temporary
condition, justifies and produces the material

conditions of their exclusion, while preventing the acquisition of rights associated with long term presence, since it does not place them within the larger space/time of the nation. The embodiment of seemingly incompatible spaces and identities is the source of their erasure, but also the source of resistance.

In response to the specific forms of exclusion and marginalization they face, second and third generations of migrants frequently draw on and transform modes of resistance and analysis originating outside of Europe and circulated in transnational discourses of diaspora, ranging from hip hop culture to women of colour feminism. Exclusionary spatio-temporal structures are remixed into alternative models that allow us to think the unthinkable: an identity that is both European and non-white/Christian.

This remixing takes place in the art and activism produced by racialized Europeans, beginning in the early 1980s with the experimental work of the Black Audio Film Collective —maybe best expressed in John Akomfrah's *The Last Angel of History* (1996), which brilliantly links Afrofuturism, a vision of the contemporaneity of past and future borne of the fundamental displacement of transatlantic slavery, the hybrid origins of hip hop, and Walter Benjamin's claim that the tradition of the oppressed teaches us that the state of exception is the rule. This activistic remixing is continued by collectives such as Kanak Attak, rejecting the logic that erases racialized Europeans between the binaries structuring progressive time and space(Orient/Occident, archaic/modern, rural/urban, fundamentalism/ enlightenment, Islam/Europe, past/future) by offensively embodying the unstable relationship between these supposed opposites; and of course remixing is everywhere in Euro hip hop, negating the spatial logic of the state through a trans-local and trans-ethnic counterdiscourse.

In Europe, the particular histories of colonialism, racism, and migration create intersections and overlaps between, in particular, black, Muslim, and Roma communities, which result in shared spaces (including the outer city, prisons, and detention centres, inner city), cultures (such as hip hop), histories, and positionalities (as not properly European). These connections are suppressed in dominant (policy-producing) discourses that assign each group a distinct representational function: Muslims appear as the internal threat posed by migration, the 'other' that is already here but remains eternally foreign; whereas

'Africans' (including black Europeans) represent the masses not yet there, pushing at the borders, the demographic (and racial) Goliath threatening to run over the European David (the prevalence of metaphors along these lines helps to normalize the extremely high death toll the EU migration regime produces on its external borders, complemented by a rapidly growing and increasingly privatized regime of mass incarceration of undocumented migrants). The Roma, finally, the quintessential European minority of colour, with a 500-year-old continental history that includes slavery and genocide, continue to face extreme violence, poverty, and exclusion, while being completely absent as a recognized presence in contemporary Europe. Instead, they are framed as not only coming from another, non-European, space, but also from another time, an idealized European past, as reflected in the centrality of 'gypsies' in continental folklore.

The discursive separation of these groups is symptomatic for the ways in which de facto intersections of communities of colour—with each other and with white Europe—are negated within the ideology of colour-blindness, which cannot allow for porous boundaries and instead has to continuously produce distinct and homogenous communities. The particular forms of exclusion produced by this system require methods of resistance that cannot always be direct, and instead have to use detours, disidentifications, and diversions in order to produce positionalities from which to break the silence around Europe's deeply racialized sense of self. This strategy of 'queering' ethnicity, practised across the continent by multi-ethnic hip hop crews, black and Muslim feminists, queer performers, urban guerrilla video artists and many others, is grounded in the shared, peculiar experience of embodying an identity that is declared impossible, even though it is lived by millions, the experience of constantly being defined as foreign to everything one is most familiar with.

This essay was first published in Vivian Paulissen et al., eds., *Remixing Europe: Migrants, Media, Representation, Imagery* (Amsterdam, 2014), pp. 76-79.

III — FRAGMENTATION AND SOLIDARITY

'NEUE HEIMAT?'
How Refugees Make Us Better Neighbours

Marina Naprushkina

July 2013
The Emergency Accommodation

The vacant school is now serving as emergency
accommodation for refugees, at least I think it is.
In any case, no one can tell me anything for certain,
and I can't be indifferent to it because I can't just
ignore it. But can I just turn up there? What would
I ask, what would I say, what exactly do I want there?
A bald man at the entrance, black, Security. Hello,
may I go in please? The director of the centre, Irina,
is unbelievably young, late twenties at most. She
covers up for her inexperience with an authoritative
appearance, that's how I perceive her. 'We do a lot
for the people here', she says, 'German classes,
sports. You want to do some drawing with the
children? A room?' Fine by her. I follow her. She
leads me into a former classroom. 'This is where
our German classes take place.' 'Fuck' is written
on the board in German. Two security staff snigger
behind our backs.

August 2013
The Room

This isn't working, I can't cope like this. How much
material do we actually need every day? And the
children are hungry too, so we need apples, choco-
late spread sandwiches, juice. Go shopping every
morning, look for material on eBay, drive through
Berlin and pick everything up. Tabletops from the
 DIY shop, chairs, shelves from friends, the room
is empty. I'm getting on everyone's nerves. But
people are starting to join in. Word has spread, more
helpers are turning up every day. Luis, awkward
with children, all thumbs, but with a heart of gold.
Or Veronika, the teacher, who gets stuck in right
from the start, or Carina, with three children at home
and other problems, who drives the whole way
across the city every day to help us. The director
and her employees eye us with suspicion; speaking
with refugees as equals is probably strange to them.
Usually, people here are just regulated and repri-
manded.

The room is small, far too small, and we spill out
into the corridors, hang up the drawings, take photos
together with the children. The next day the photos
are gone. The children took them off the walls to keep
them.

MRS MERKEL

I promised Salima I'd go with her to the authorities today. We meet there at nine o'clock. The waiting room is full of people, many of them have brought the whole family with them, children of all ages are waiting patiently too. The only attraction in the waiting room is the water fountain. The children go there often and fetch water.

Salima joins the queue to take a number. That goes relatively quickly. We watch the monitor. It shows the numbers in the queue, and the room. Salima has her baby with her. The little girl is fast asleep on her lap.

Salima is a bit worked up. They've been told they're being moved out of Berlin. She doesn't want that to happen. She asked me to come along and talk to the official in charge.

I don't know what's awaiting us here either. I asked Salima to bring the newspaper article with her. The article describes the story of their persecution. Salima's husband was tortured. Since Salima and Usman left Chechnya, their relatives who stayed behind have been receiving threats.

Salima's lawyer is in Berlin; that's why she's afraid to leave.

We're constantly looking at the monitor, comparing the numbers. They're not shown in order. Similar numbers appear, but never the four numbers on Salima's slip of paper. Two hours have passed already. Salima breastfeeds the baby. The waiting room is full. A smell of food starts to waft through the room. I realize I'm hungry. There's a catering company next door, which has put huge billboards up right at the entrance, using photos of their dishes to advertise. They use the same building for their cooking. For the people who have to wait here for hours on end, it can't be much fun seeing the billboards and hungrily smelling the food.

'Marina, go and ask when it's our turn', Salima asks me. 'Last time I ended up waiting for five hours, they simply forgot me.'

I take what Salima says with a pinch of salt. Perhaps she simply missed her number last time. But after waiting for three hours, I start getting impatient too. I join the queue and wait, it moves very slowly. A man pushes his way to the front.

'Who speaks Russian?' he asks the people behind the large reception desk in Russian. No one responds. A woman comes darting out from one of the rooms. 'What do you want here?' she snaps at the man in Russian.

'My wife's not very well', he says shyly.

I recognize the young man, he and his wife had been waiting next to us. He looks about eighteen. She's very young too, heavily pregnant.

'What's wrong with her? Does she have a headache?' the woman grumbles at him.

'She's in pain, her tummy…'

'Yes, and? Is she about to have the baby right now?' she interrupts him at once. 'What do you expect me to do? Do you think I'm going to let you go to the front because of that?'

I can't take it anymore. 'Why are you talking to him like that, who do you think you are?' I ask in Russian, immediately regretting not speaking to her in German. But I wanted her to know that I'd understood everything.

'And who are you to tell me how I should behave?' she snarls, quickly disappearing back into her room. The young man looks around and goes too.

Five minutes later the woman comes back out again. 'There's a baby on its way in here', she announces loudly in German to her colleagues behind the counter. 'I've called an ambulance'.

I reach the front of the queue and go up to an employee. I explain that we've been waiting for our number to be called for three hours.

'It always takes a while', he says, looking at me. He wants to simply get rid of me. I explain that we can't wait any longer, that the woman is tired, and the baby too.

'Are you accompanying someone? Show me the number', he says. The situation that refugees have someone with them is new to him.

He types something in the computer. 'Yes, the number was taken out again', he says. 'How strange.'

'What do you mean, taken out? How's that possible?' I become impatient.

'Wait a moment, I'll call my colleague.' He picks up the phone and makes a quick call, then he stands up. 'Please come with me.'

Salima and I follow the man. He takes us to the third floor. There's another waiting room there. 'They'll call you up. Please wait here', he says and leaves.

We wait. I'm annoyed. The same people who were waiting with us downstairs are sitting here too. I imagine there being more small waiting rooms on every floor in this high-rise building. You keep getting moved up a floor, only to have to wait again. You never get seen to.

After half an hour, I knock on a door to one of the rooms.

'Yes, I know you're there, but it takes time. I'm already processing your paperwork', a young woman at the desk says to me, somewhat irritated.

'But I need to speak to you first', I explain. I want to avoid us just being given some signed documents here in the corridor, without being able to speak to anyone.

'What's it about then?' the woman asks.

'I've brought a few documents along. I need to show them to you.' I go into the room and take out the papers.

The woman listens to me. When I show her the newspaper article, her colleague becomes curious too. 'Is it OK if we take a copy of that?' he asks.

'And who will make the decision then?' I ask.

'A computer program. The program assigns the refugees to the various federal states. It shows where they have to go. We can't change it.'

'But there's got to be someone who can override the computer?' I comment.

'Try contacting Mrs Merkel. She's very busy though.'

'Mrs Merkel? What do you mean by that?' I get the impression they're trying to wind me up.

'Mrs Susanne Merkel, on the sixth floor. I'll write it down for you.'

'Can I get a meeting with her?'

'No, but you can send her a letter.'

Salima is then called into the room; she'd been waiting outside the whole time.

Salima has to sign lots of documents to confirm she received the money for the next month.

'Marina, please can you ask her whether I'll get the money for winter clothing', she says to me.

I ask.

'No, not today. Maybe at the next appointment.'

The next appointment is at the end of November. They are perfectly aware that, by then, the family will have moved.

October 2013
Questions to Centre Management

We need to talk to centre management. The mood is sour, we're being bossed around. What we're seeing and what we're hearing from the refugees is not compatible with our impression of humane accommodation. It's unacceptable that the people are treated like this here, after all the trauma they've gone through. Not here and not on our watch. Every day, the mothers come to me with reports of new problems. Why are there only five operational washing machines for almost three hundred residents, why is there only lukewarm water in the showers, why are the toilets always dirty and broken, no soap, no toilet paper, why is there no lounge, no internet, why does the mere sight of the food make me want to puke? And all of that for almost thirty euros per person per day, paid to the operator by the federal state government. The standards need to be met, we demand. Something here is going drastically wrong. The service doesn't correspond with the payment at all, even a blind person could see that. Why's no one monitoring it? We need to sort it all out.

JOURNEY

On 25 November, Salima has her appointment with the authorities. Salima suspects she won't be getting another extension for Berlin. The family will be relocated. That was the decision, you can't do anything about it. Nothing at all.

Salima is in a panic, she doesn't want to leave, she likes Berlin, she has friends here, her relatives live in Berlin too. I wrote a letter to the authorities, requesting the head of the department to allow the family to stay in Berlin.

There are health reasons that speak against a relocation, there are social contacts that the family has already made, and there's our initiative, which is willing to help the family.

I read the letter out to Salima and her eyes lit up, full of hope. I did warn her that it's extremely unlikely that it'll be of any use.

And indeed: I soon receive a very formal refusal to my request.

On 24 November, Sunday evening, one day before the appointment, Salima rings me. She's calling from the hospital, she needs an interpreter. At first I think Salima herself is ill, but it's the children. Three of the seven children are ill, with fever and vomiting. 'It's an infection', the nurse on the phone explains. 'The children need to be separated from the other children so they don't pass it on.' I explain that there are seven children in the family and that they all live in the same room.

What's more, over a hundred children live in the centre; preventing contact between the children would be impossible. But it's no use. Salima's not allowed to stay in the hospital and has to go back to the centre with the children.

Back then, I wasn't aware that they object to keeping refugees in hospital, children included. The authorities want to avoid the costs.

Early this morning, Salima calls. She's on her way from the paediatrician to the authorities. She has a doctor's note from the hospital and a letter from the paediatrician with her. The doctor says that one child still probably needs to go to hospital today. It should therefore be clear to the authorities that the family can't travel today. Salima doesn't ring me again after that and I assume that she has received her extension for Berlin.

In the afternoon, Malika approaches me. The first thing she says is that she helped Salima pack everything up today. 'Salima has already left', she tells me.

I'm speechless.

'What do you mean, left? The children are ill.' I can't believe it.

After nine that evening, my mobile rings. It's

Salima. She tells me they're on the train. They
need to change trains again, but that's as much
as they know.
'How come?' I ask. 'Don't you have an address
of where you need to go? Did no one from the
authority tell you how to get there? Have a look
in your paperwork, the address of the new centre
must be there somewhere', I say in despair.
At nine in the evening, it's too late to ask anyone
at the authority.
We agree that she'll let me know when she
arrives at the final stop. Half an hour, later
my phone rings again. Salima hands her mobile
to someone else. There's a woman who's willing
to help on the other end. She says she's got a
car, but she can only take two people. 'But there
are nine... It's still another ten kilometres to
where they need to be. I'll ask the police if they
can take them.' The lady sounds friendly and
concerned.
It rings again, the same woman's voice, 'The
police say they're not a taxi service. But they
could have some humanity!' She gets upset.
'It's arctic here, there's no heating in the railway
station', she describes the situation. 'The children
are freezing! I'll see if any buses are still running.
If not, I'll go back to the police.' She calls again a
short time later. 'The last bus left ages ago. But
I'll sort this out.' I'm annoyed. They decide

to send a family with sick, young children on their way, well aware that they can no longer reach their destination by public transport!

An hour later I phone Salima and ask where they are now. 'I don't know, Marina, I think we're in a police station.' She passes the phone over.

'Hello. With whom am I speaking?' a male voice enquires. 'With whom am I speaking?' I ask back. 'Where are the family now?'

I'm told that the family have already arrived in the emergency accommodation. I ask for a paediatrician and explain that the children are ill.

'We've got a doctor here. We've got all that's needed here. It's all automatic here', the man says. It doesn't sound caring. More like in a military barracks. I google the refugee centre.

Lots of reports pop up with catchwords like: hunger strike, deportation camp, four hundred and fifty residents, hundreds of unsupervised children, a camp in the woods behind bars. The most recent report is from March 2013. Let's hope that something has been donwe since this media furore. The centre is actually very large, it's located just outside a small village consisting of three roads. The nearest lawyer? I do a search. There's one forty-three kilometres away. But that's a different district. That means you'd need to get authorization

from the authorities every time you wanted
to visit the lawyer. The same would apply if you
needed medical assistance or a psychologist.
The statement from the authorities that the
refugees have access to medical and legal
assistance at all locations does not correspond
with reality. How are four hundred and fifty
refugees expected to get by at this location?
How can they reach the public if something
happens?

I call Salima, her mobile is switched off.
Battery or credit gone.

December 2013
Replanning

Mediation meeting with the operator of the centre,
organized by the local council. A spectacular
failure, despite a professional moderator and
the presence of the Mayor for Social Affairs.
The reason: the managers didn't show up, and
the representatives of the operator of the centre
have been ordered not to reach an agreement
with us. A waste of time, everyone is annoyed.

We had to give up the former studio in
the centre. The bar 'Neue Heimat' is making its
premises available, only two hundred metres
away from the emergency accommodation.
A perfect location. Everyone will find their way
there easily. The first events: handing out warm
clothes and material donations. For the 'Christmas
party' we rock the whole street. Three shops have
agreed to make their premises available for the
party. It works: people come flocking down the
street from the centre, more than a hundred adults
and children turn up.

People do arts and crafts in 'Dunja', a clown
entertains the children in the 'Kulturbremse' and
there's music and a buffet in the 'Neue Heimat'.
The little ones have fun. Excitement grows,
they wait for the presents and push and shove.
Udo, disguised as Father Christmas, is surrounded
by parents and children and barely survives the
gift giving.

AFTER NEW YEAR

Salima comes to Berlin today and asks if I can interpret at the meeting with the lawyer tomorrow. I agree. I'm glad Salima gave me enough notice this time. That was never the case before.

The meeting is at five in the afternoon in Kreuzberg. We travel there together from Moabit. At four, Salima is waiting for me at the entrance to 'Zeeman'. The shop always used to be our meeting point. But Salima's not on her own. A young woman is standing beside her. They're surrounded by a bunch of children. OK, I think, we really need to get going now with this whole gang, otherwise we're going to be late.

Salima's little son recognizes me and shakes my hand with great pleasure. We chat in the bus. I exchange a few words with the woman who came with Salima. She's called Seda and has her three children with her. Her husband's in prison in a detention centre.

'I was at the lawyer's today', she says, 'but a Chechen woman who promised she'd come with me to the doctor's to get the certificates didn't turn up', she explains despondently. She seems exhausted. She's wearing a headscarf, a long black skirt, and pink trainers. She's very thin. Her hands, the fingers are big and bony, like a man's. She tries to keep the children together.

The older daughter, who looks about six years old, is good and sticks with the mother. The younger daughter is in the pushchair. The son, who must be about four, bounds around the bus the whole time. Seda tries, in vain, to calm him down.

'Mohamed, come here, come here right now!' The boy doesn't listen.

The bus is full, we fight our way to the exit and hurry to the underground station.

There we wait for the lift. Three women, two pushchairs, five young children. The announcement in the lift warns that the door is closing: 'Vorsicht, die Tür schließt'.

The children laugh. 'Tür sch... schlih.... Tür schißt!' they all yell together, laughing.

'Tür schließt', I say loudly and clearly. Five beaming pairs of eyes look at me.

'Tür schließt', we repeat together, then everyone laughs again.

We're on the platform. The train arrives. Salima rummages around in her bag. She can't find the ticket. We get a new one. The train leaves without us. Then Seda starts looking for her ticket. She eventually finds one. I ask her to show it to me. Long since expired. I go back to the ticket machine, we get on the next train. I check the time, it's going to be tight. The train is full. Salima finds somewhere to sit near the entrance.

Seda parks her pushchair at the door and keeps the children together. All the children have got bottles of bubbles, which they're constantly throwing onto the floor, then they pour the soapy water over each other. The four-year-old jumps around wildly, runs to the door, presses the button and is delighted when the door opens. His mother tries to catch him and bring him back. The same thing happens at every stop. 'It's so difficult to cope on your own with three young children. And this one here', she points to the four-year-old, 'doesn't even listen to me', she says with a weary smile.

'Yes, he's certainly got a lot of energy', I say.

'He'll be the death of her before the father comes out of prison', Salima comments.

'How are you getting on in the new centre then?' I ask. 'What do you do all day?' I ask Salima.

'We're doing well, Marina', she smiles. 'We don't do anything. Sleep, eat, clean up. It would be great if it could stay like that, if the authorities were to just forget we're here.'

Salima shows me some photos of the flat. ' On the fourth floor', she says proudly. A high-rise. The flat looks like a lift, empty, with a few pieces of furniture.

'That's our bedroom. And this is the kitchen. That room's still completely empty', Salima explains. The happy faces of the family members can be seen in all of the photos. They pose in the half-empty flat in front of the few items of furniture. On the large black sofa in one, in front of the cupboard on the next.

We go a few stops on the underground.

'Guten Tag', the young son suddenly says to me, smiling. 'Guten Tag', I respond.

We change trains, lug the pushchairs down the steps, get on another train and get off it again. Salima doesn't know the way. I have a quick look to see where we need to go. We're late. I lead the way, the women and children follow behind. It's Friday, Friday evening, I worry that the lawyer won't wait for us. But we're in luck.

'It's unlikely that the relocation to Poland will go ahead. The deadline for the transfer has almost expired', the lawyer explains. First of all, the family shouldn't worry. Salima can't believe it. She's very fearful of being sent to Poland. There's a risk that her husband will be killed by Chechen agents there, she says. Usman is afraid of being deported and can't sleep at night because of it. His name is on the Chechen government's wanted list. The lawyer shows me the list. A long list.

Salima keeps asking what to do when the letter about the relocation arrives. 'No, it won't be coming now', the lawyer assures her.

Seda and the children are waiting for us in

the waiting room. The room is barely recognizable. The books and toys are strewn all over the floor, the floor is wet: the remainder of the soapy water.

We put our coats on. At the last minute, Mohamed, the four-year-old, decides he needs the toilet. According to his mother, he can manage on his own. I show him where the toilet is and switch the light on. He goes in and locks the door. After a while we hear crying. The children all run to the toilet door.

The little boy has locked himself in and can't open the door again. Oh no, I think, that's the last thing we need. We speak to Mohamed through the door and tell him what and where he needs to turn. I go to the secretary and ask if she's got a key for the toilet door. She doesn't. We manage to open the door with a five cent coin. We leave the law office. Salima is in good spirits. Good news at last.

The following Tuesday, the lawyer writes to me, 'It's absolutely essential that the family looks out for their post and reports immediately if they receive a yellow letter. Unfortunately, just before the deadline, the Federal Office made an application in Poland. The Polish authorities have declared their consent to take back the family.'

MOBILE PHONE

My mobile won't stop ringing. Once, then three times… six missed calls in the last ten minutes. Salima. I know what she's going to ask. I don't have anything new to report at the moment. The lawyer hasn't replied.

The appeal against being returned to Poland was lodged. However, it does not have suspensive effect. No one can guarantee that the police won't turn up tomorrow. The family need to hold out for another two months. Then the deadline by which Germany can send the family to Poland will be up. The lawyer promised Salima she'd notify us immediately when the date for deportation is entered into the file.

But Salima doesn't want to count on that, she believes nothing. Rightly so.

The woman is anxious, she's already had a nervous breakdown. She calls even though she's got nothing to report, and I've got nothing to report either.

The mobile rings again.

'You're doing it wrong', Udo tells me. 'Pick up and say you can't talk today, that you'll give her a ring tomorrow. Not later, but tomorrow.'

It rings again. I go to the bedroom and close the door behind me. 'Hello Salima. How are you all?'

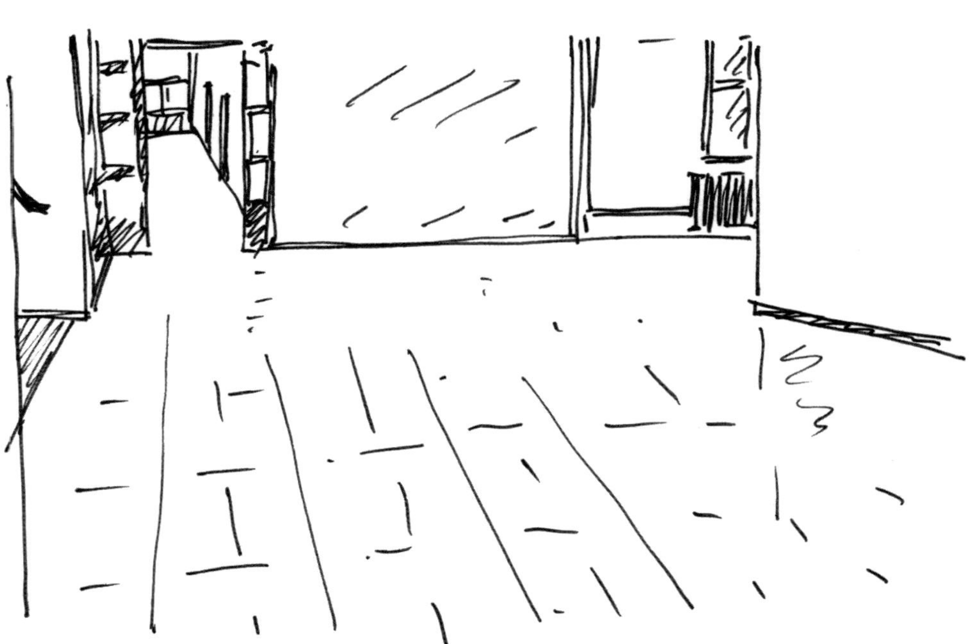

SIX FORTY-TWO

Half asleep, it takes me a moment to work out what's going on. My mobile. It's vibrating somewhere nearby. I quickly reach for it. I open it. Salima's calling. I close it again. Call ended, the irritating noise is gone. I check the time: six forty-two. I hope I didn't wake anyone up. I'm in the hotel room. We arrived here around midnight last night. It's the long-awaited family trip to visit Udo's father in Stuttgart. And after a long train journey, all anyone wants is a lie-in.

It vibrates again. Open cover, close cover, mobile to one side, close eyes again. After the third call, I'm wide awake and pretty annoyed. Salima never really paid much attention to the time. Sometimes she'll ring ridiculously early, other times she'll ring in the middle of the night.

This time it'll probably be about the 'travel permit'. Salima wants to go to Berlin again to visit her lawyer. But does that really need to be sorted out at six in the morning? Annoyed, I pick up, 'Good morning, Salima. What's up?'

'Marina', her voice trembles, 'the police are here. "Deport". We're being deported.' She sobs.

'What?!' I jump out of bed and run to the toilet, closing the door behind me. I don't want to wake everyone up.

'The police are here', Salima says. 'Marina,

I don't get it, the lawyer said she'd give us advance notice before we get deported.'

'Salima, the lawyer wrote to me yesterday saying that everything's fine', I say, knowing of course that it doesn't make a bit of difference now.

'Hasan's not at home', Salima says. 'Tell them.' She passes her phone on.

I tell the policeman that one of the children isn't at home.

'Please ask the mother where the child is', he says.

'Salima, where's the child?' I ask, hoping I won't receive an answer.

'With relatives. I don't know where they live though. They took him with them and will be bringing him back soon', Salima says.

I interpret.

'The family will be travelling to Poland today', the policeman explains to me. 'Tell her they need to pack everything up. And ask where the child is.'

'I already told you that the mother doesn't know where the child is', I say. 'I can't do anything else, all I can do is interpret what the woman just told me.'

'Then we'll do without your interpreting services in future. We'll find out where the child is', he tells me. 'How are you going to do that then?' I ask.

'You needn't worry about that, we're resource-
ful.' He hangs up.

Udo has woken up.

'Salima's being deported', I say. 'Damn it! The
deadline's in three days' time... the lawyer didn't
give us any advance warning.'

I check the time. Only seven. Just like they said.
The police usually come for deportation between
five and seven. When the lawyer opens her office
at ten this morning, she'll have one less client.

'Tell Salima she has the right to remain silent',
Udo tells me.

I dial her number, hoping she'll pick up.

'Salima, you don't have to say anything to them.
They'll have to put an end to their operation if
your child's not there', I explain to her.

'Marina, they're saying the children and I have
to go to Poland. My husband's got to stay here
and wait for Hasan. Can you tell them we'll make
our own way there all together once Hasan's
back?' Salima doesn't cry, but she sounds very
demoralized. Usually, that never happens to her.

'Salima, they're not allowed to separate you.
Put the police on.'

'You're not allowed to separate the family,
you're aware of that', I tell the policeman.

'That's not our decision, we're just executing
what was decided by the immigration authority.'

'The immigration authority didn't order you to

separate the family, though', I say.

Udo takes the phone out of my hand. 'Listen here, what's your name? We're going to make a disciplinary complaint. It will be against you personally, because you're the one executing it. Do you hear me? Hello! Hello?'

They've hung up. I dial Salima's number again. Voicemail. Have they taken her phone away?

We need to be at Udo's father's place for breakfast soon. We get dressed. The phone rings again. It's Salima's sister. She lives in Berlin. I don't know whether or not I should pick up. What if someone's intercepting it? What if the child's with her? I pick up. She already knows what's going on.

'Can you go to the law firm as soon as it opens? Straight away, with the child', I say.

'Hasan's not with us', she replies. Just don't tell me where he is, I think.

Udo's family are sitting around the table, Gundolf in a suit with a bow tie, Greta's dressed smartly too. It's a real pleasure for them both to have us here. Breakfast. A beautiful, sunny morning. Bread rolls, pretzels, jam and strawberries. Then the morning verse the family say in prayer. Something rings in my trouser pocket. I excuse myself and get up. Greta looks at me, but doesn't say anything. I struggle with myself briefly. I ought to explain the situation from this morning.

'Marina, they've gone!' Salima says. The telephone cuts off. Money or battery gone. Delight. I return to the table. The phone buzzes again. Salima's sister. 'The police have gone', she tells me.

We eat. Udo takes care of the entertainment. I'm barely able to follow the conversation and think that it'll soon be ten o'clock and I need to phone the lawyer. Who knows what else is going to happen today.

I get up and go to a different room. The secretary picks up.

'Ms N. is at court today, she'll be back in the office this afternoon. But I'll pass it all on. What you've achieved there is wonderful!'

I go back to the table. Greta is really upset. A breakfast like this needs to be perfect. It can't be interrupted. Twelve o'clock. I help Greta prepare lunch. My phone buzzes. The lawyer. I tell her about this morning.

'I already know', she interrupts, 'can we keep it brief?'

I ask her how soon the police might come back and whether it's also possible for an operation like that to be carried out at the weekend. 'I don't know. They're booking seats on buses to Poland. As soon as more seats become available... I don't know why they came today. There wasn't anything in the file.'

Greta is peeling asparagus. Salima calls every few minutes. I try to find an excuse to disappear. Again, I don't succeed in telling Greta who I've been on the phone to this whole time and why.

'I'm just going outside for a moment, Greta, you've got such beautiful flowers in the garden', I say. On the phone, Salima is agitated and doesn't know what to do. She's thinking about travelling to Berlin.

I call the lawyer.

'She can travel to Berlin, but please make sure she doesn't take the train', she says. It's too dangerous, because they might catch her on the way.

Then it's lunchtime. Greta lays the table. Udo's supposed to be helping. But he does it all wrong. Greta isn't happy.

'The pattern needs to be the right way round', she says, turning all the plates around. Two forks, two spoons, a rest for the knives.

'I'm going to make you a proposal. I don't know what you're going to make of it. Please just switch off your mobile.' Greta can't bear it anymore.

We eat. Asparagus with potatoes and boiled ham. Udo's phone starts buzzing in his trouser pocket. Salima's got his number too.

The dinner goes on for what feels like an eternity. Greta wants it to be a celebration. Outside it's raining, my daughter starts to get grumpy. I seize the opportunity: the journey yesterday was exhausting, the child needs to sleep. We'll eat the dessert after dinner instead. I'm allowed to leave.

I've only just arrived in the hotel room when my phone rings again.

Nummer	Raum	Nummer	Raum
2505	0001	2012	0311
2013	0312	1519	0422
2505	0001	1015	0408
1015	0403	1019	0408

1034 Bitte zum Antragsannahme

CHURCH

'Marina, where are you at the moment?' Salima sounds tired.

'We've been walking around outside since first thing this morning. The neighbour of the friends we've been staying with said she's going to get the police because the children are too loud for her and I'm scared they're going to take us away. I just managed to get the children dressed. And then out of there. We can't go back. Marina, I've decided we're going to go to the church now.'

It's two in the afternoon, I arrive home, send my daughter to her flute lesson.

I ask Udo to come with me.

He sends a message to the internal group, telling them we're heading off and that anyone who wants can join us. No responses. Just as we're about to set off, it starts raining. Very heavily. Then hail. I call Salima. I hope she took shelter, with her seven children, before the rain started. Salima doesn't pick up. And then she does. 'Yes, we're waiting', she says patiently.

Once it stops raining, we set off. A police van with four police officers inside is parked in front of the church. What are they doing here, of all places? Lunch break? One of the police officers is sitting on the back seat, eating a kebab.

Salima is sitting with her husband and children

on a park bench. We wait and wait, keeping
an eye on the police van at all times. I ask Salima
whether she's eaten anything today. No.

I buy some bread rolls. The children wolf down
the food.

The parents are at their wits' end. Especially
the father. He just stares down at the ground in
silence. Almost an hour passes. The police van
is still there. Did the police intercept the email?
Salima laughs nervously.

Eventually, the police van drives away, the
family go inside the church. There's just an older
man sitting behind a table. We tell him that the
family are seeking asylum in this church. The
man stares at the ground. 'There's no one there,
I need to lock up the church at six o'clock', he
says. He doesn't want anything to do with the
matter. Apparently he can't inform anyone else
either.

I find the vicar's telephone number in a church
brochure that's on display. She picks up and isn't
sure at first, she promises to ring back. We wait.
I get some chairs for the children and the parents.

Salima looks around. 'This is the first time I've
ever been in a church', she says.

Another half an hour passes. The children are
tired, they rest their heads on the tabletops and
sleep sitting up. Salima breastfeeds the baby.

After an hour, the vicar finally returns my call.

'The family need to leave... I can't help them. Everywhere is full. I'm actually off today. I've been advised to call the police.'

But then she promises to carry out one last attempt after all. We wait. We're anxious. What if she actually calls the police?

Another forty minutes pass. Church bells ring. It's six o'clock. The older man gets up out of his chair.

'I need to close up now', he says. 'You need to leave.' We look at him. We don't say anything. The man brings the sign in from the street and sits back down in his chair. The vicar then arrives on her bike. First of all, she stays outside the entrance to the church and makes a phone call.

We have no idea what's going to happen. Church asylum or police station? She comes in, shakes hands with everyone. She looks around, 'Have the children already had something to eat?' she asks me.

December 2014
Work

We want to remain independent, we don't apply
for any grants, be they government or private,
we don't want to become part of the 'structure'
and administration. That's what makes us special,
what makes us strong. This way, we can main-
tain a critical distance from politics, the state,
church, social organizations.

We are financed by flea markets and solidarity
concerts. We pay for tickets, legal costs, birthday
presents, sports lessons for the children, food.
The network is getting bigger, a lot can be
achieved. But I want more. The people need to
come together more closely. Both sides can
be enriched by it. I've had the feeling for a while
now that the 'German' neighbours learn a
lot from their new neighbours and benefit from
the initiative. Working in the initiative does
something to us. You learn something new
every day. Especially for young students coming
to Berlin, the initiative is the best place to
become integrated here. They meet people, they
break down inhibitions, they understand how
Germany functions for those people who aren't
in possession of a German passport. They look
discrimination in the face and learn how to speak
out against it. And they find new friends from
different cultures. Sometimes even partners.
The group mingles, people go out together, cook
for each other, celebrate birthdays.

Another general meeting. Everyone together,
it's so tight you're almost sitting on each other's

laps. It's interpreted into a number of languages. I'm moved, because so much has been done and everyone's really focused and full of enthusiasm. I ask Mohamed why he comes to us. 'To make friends', he says, without a moment's hesitation.

ALLAH

I visit Salima. More than a month has passed since the family moved into the parish hall. Salima and Usman are still very unsettled. They find it hard to believe that they are safe here, that the police won't turn up. The atmosphere is still very tense.

Salima makes tea for me.

'Oh, Marina', she says, resting her head on her fist. 'It is what it is. You can't do anything to change it. Nothing at all. That's what I always tell Usman when he starts thinking too much again. It will be however Allah wants it to be. It's all His will.'

I take a deep breath and say nothing. It took a lot of effort to get the family to safety, furnish the flat, arrange money, find clothing, register the children with the school, come to an agreement with the church... Allah certainly wouldn't have been able to do all of that. Almost ten people from our group are still working on the case. Salima looks at me. 'And Allah brought you to us', she says as an afterthought.

The above texts are a selection from: Marina Naprushkina, *Neue Heimat? Wie Flüchtlinge uns zu besseren Nachbarn machen* (Berlin, Munich and Vienna, 2015).

THE UNENDING ENIGMAS OF ARRIVAL Series 1—3
John Akomfrah

III – FRAGMENTATION AND SOLIDARITY

pp. 229–231
John Akomfrah
The Unending Enigmas of Arrival Series 1, 2018, triptych
Copyright John Akomfrah, Courtesy Smoking Dogs Films
and Lisson Gallery

pp. 233–235
John Akomfrah
The Unending Enigmas of Arrival Series 2, 2018, triptych
Copyright John Akomfrah, Courtesy Smoking Dogs Films
and Lisson Gallery

pp. 237–239
John Akomfrah
The Unending Enigmas of Arrival Series 3, 2018, triptych
Copyright John Akomfrah, Courtesy Smoking Dogs Films
and Lisson Gallery

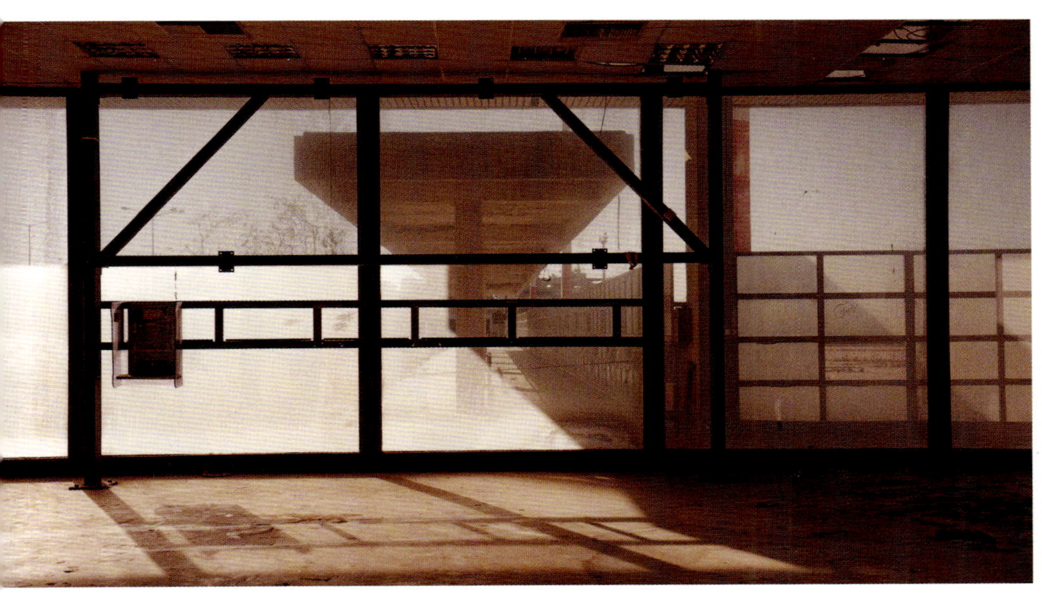

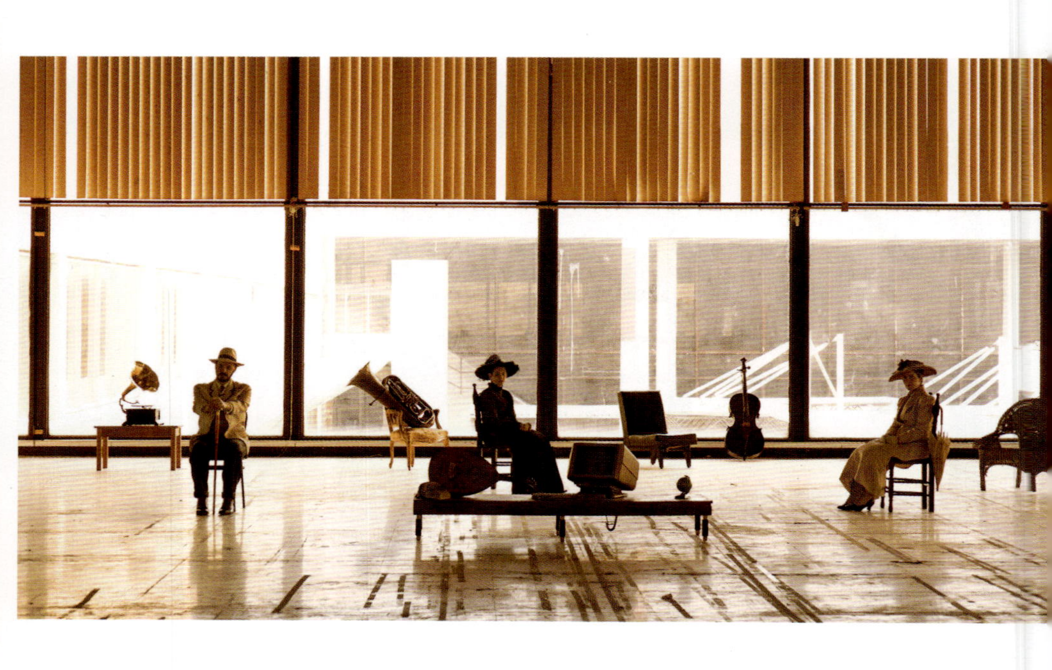

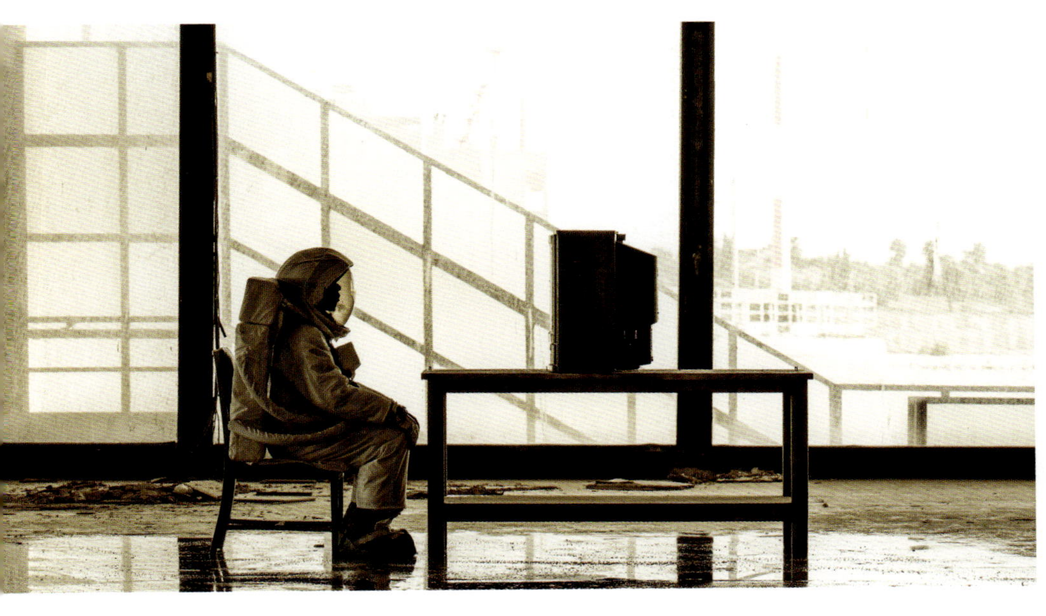

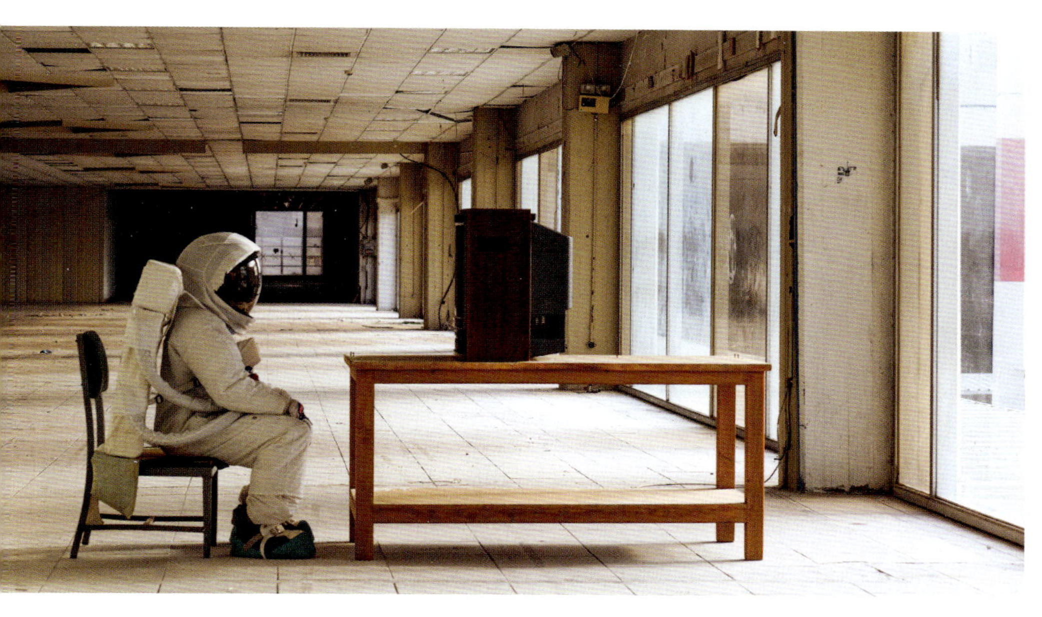

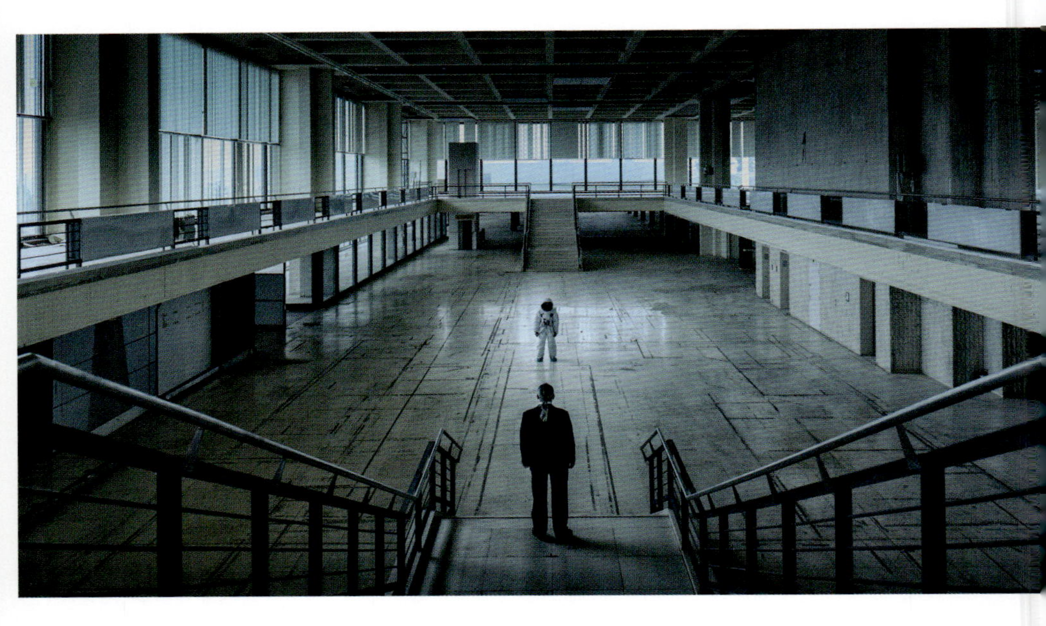

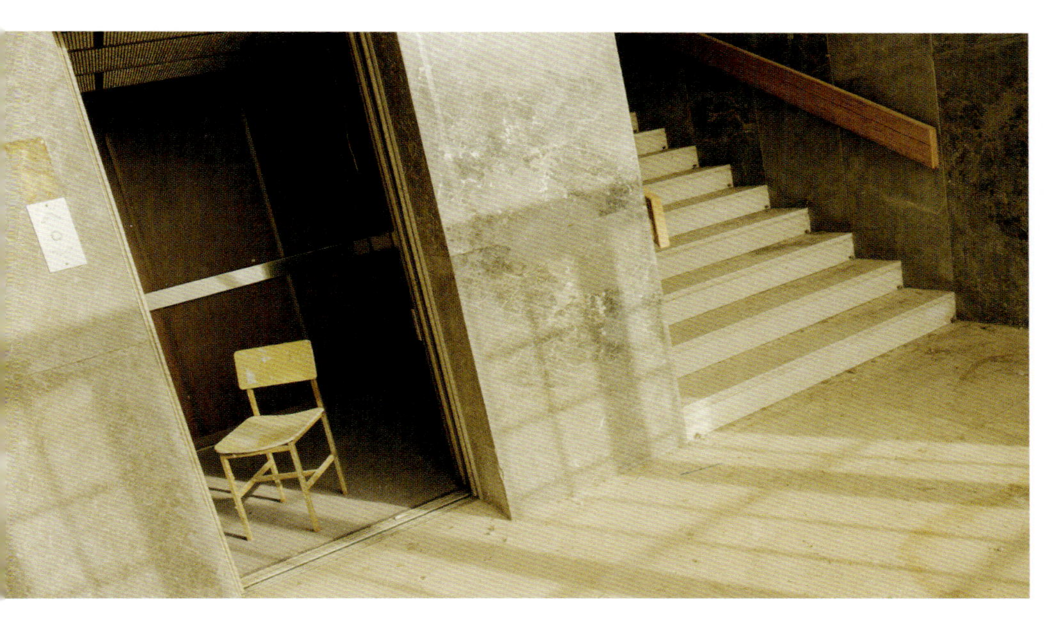

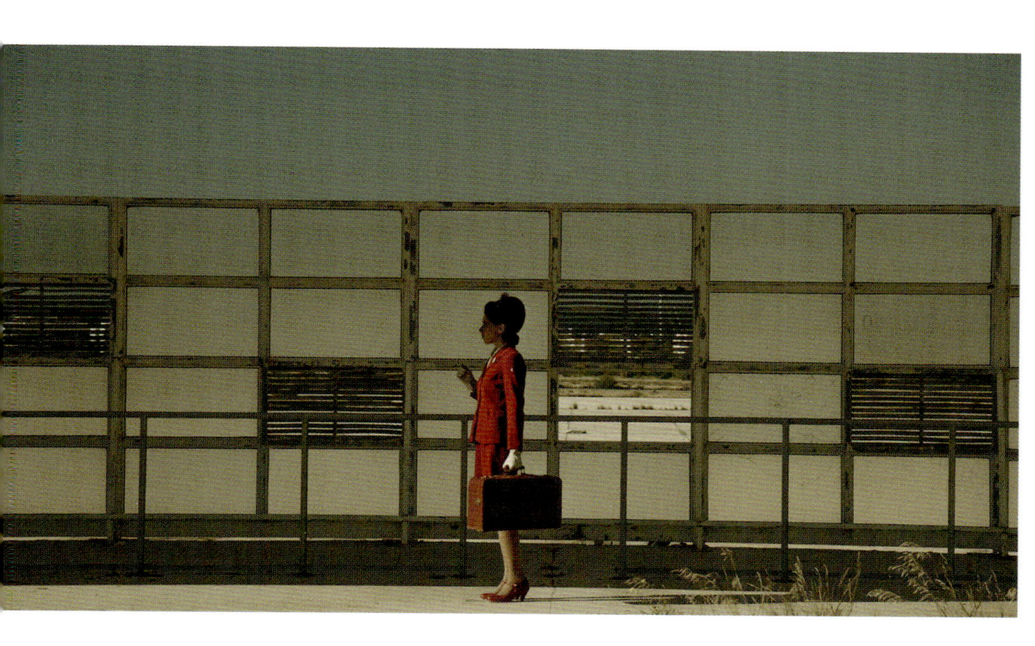

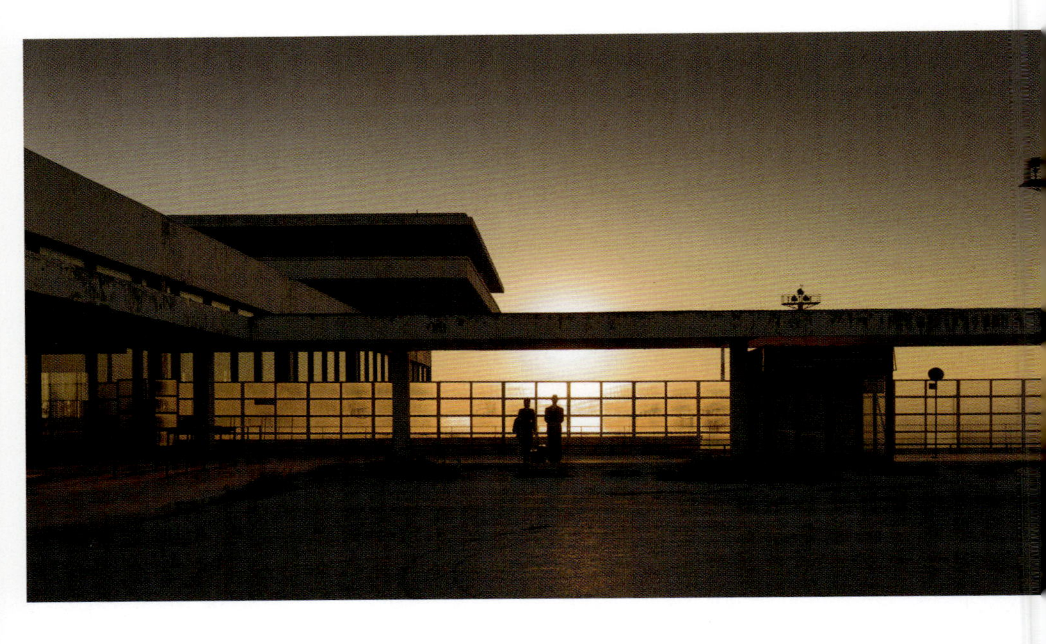

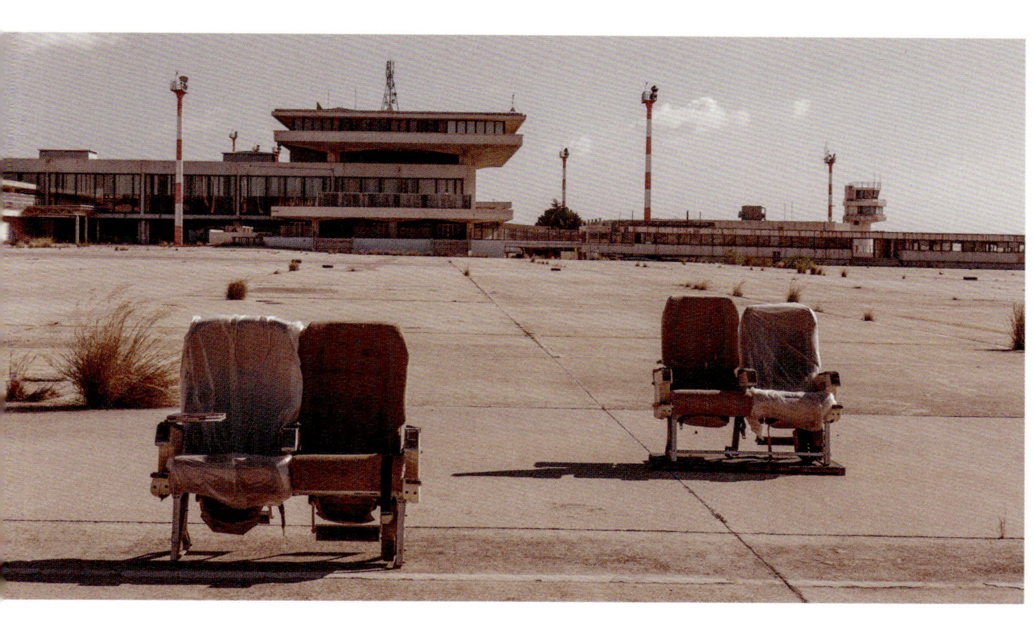

COURAGEOUS CITIZENS: EPILOGUE

Katherine Watson

COURAGEOUS CITIZENS

An epilogue is reflective by nature, it looks back and 'wraps up'. However, it should also bring learning to the future and look to tomorrow, as much as to yesterday. The legacy upon which it reflects is both a celebration of those who shaped that legacy and a gift to those who can learn, be inspired by, and grow from it. The past ten years since the first European Cultural Foundation Princess Margriet Award for Culture have been marked by economic, environmental, and democratic crises; by tragedy, conflict, and an ever-increasing acceleration of movement—ideas, goods, and people constantly in motion, intersecting and, all too often, colliding. In the face of all of this global upheaval, the courage and the determination of global citizens and of cultural change-makers has shone out with a determination to find a better way and to shape a future that is fairer and more respectful of both people and the planet we share. Thankfully, the stories pressed between the two covers of this book are just a few examples of the abundance of good ideas that are out there and are greater-than-self philosophies from people who face common struggles and share a common purpose. They are not about 'I', but about 'we'. The European Cultural Foundation's task is to support, celebrate, and champion these stories.

The life and work of Stuart Hall, one of the first laureates, so fully embodied the spirit of the Princess Margriet Award for Culture. Stuart Hall eloquently wrote about the power that comes from walking in someone's shoes—even for a little while. Seeing the world through different eyes ensures that our own eyes are not blinkered and our minds are open to more inclusive realities: 'But this experience of, as it were, experiencing oneself from the outside, as another—an other—sort of person next door is uncanny.' Our world is sorely in need of empathy and of re-discovering our place in the 'global civil parade' (Pascal Gielen) which is such a wonderful metaphor for our bonds across space, time, and difference. In this parade we need the courage to care for and lift up others when they no longer have the power or spirit to do so themselves.

Despite the waning (in some places) of the crises that reached their zenith ten years ago, in many ways and for many people, things have not changed. In fact they are even more acute. Forced migration, rooted in either economic, political or environmental causes and disaster, persists—and our response to the movement of people 'lesser' than ourselves has often been unkind. Hope for a better future has been taken over by despair. Open doors harshly closed. Conflicts wage on and tear apart communities long after these cruelties have faded from wider media and public attention.

Through it all, courageous citizens hold firm to our values of inclusion, democracy, freedom, openness. Courage—against all odds.

Courageous citizens build courageous institutions, shape courageous politicians, courageous businesses, courageous philanthropists. Risk-takers who affirm that we are in this muddle together and it is only together that we will find our way out. Courage in both small acts and in big and bold statements have joined in the parade. They have entered the fray with ideas, words, images, music.

The laureates of the past ten years are all exemplary of this idea of courageous citizenship. Citizenship that does not rest on national identity and the divisiveness that it can breed, but on responsibility and the belief in global citizenship that plays out on a local level. A citizen is every person who lives in any place— village, town or city—and who is committed to contributing to that place, to its liveability and its resilience. A citizen may have just arrived, be moving through, or have taken their first breath in a place—but for whatever length of time they share and shepherd that place, it is the care of others around them and the understanding that we are interdependent beings that is paramount.

In our increasingly fragmented communities, we know that this is not the case for all citizens—at least not now—but it will take the courage of some to reach over fissures and re-forge the humane links that have been shattered.

The hundreds of nominees of the Princess Margriet Award for Culture over the years represent many hundreds more and every laureate has passionately acknowledged that the award is the result of the myriad of people around them—they are shining examples among many.

We are sincerely grateful to all of the nominators, the jury members, and the communities that have nurtured the laureates of the past ten years. They have shown us just how much culture really matters.

As a foundation we are committed to using our resources to contribute to transformational change—change that can only happen by supporting as many courageous citizens and cultural acts as we can—and to inviting them all to join the 'global civil

parade'. Democracy and philanthropy need imagination and we
have so much to learn from the courageous citizens around us.

The European Cultural Foundation has grown and thrived, rooted
in our own legacy—from our founders more than sixty years
ago who firmly believed that Europe needed more than coal and
steel to rebuild the war-torn continent. This torch was willingly
and skilfully received and held aloft by HRH Princess Margriet
of the Netherlands, in whose name this award has been created.
All our laureates are a tribute to this legacy and a beacon of
hope for the future.

Katherine Watson joined the European Cultural Foundation in 2006 and has been
Director since 2010.

Borderland Foundation

COURAGEOUS CITIZENS

How can the memory of heritage and historical experience be helpful in creating a culture of solidarity in a world of deepening divisions, inequality, and exclusion? These and other questions were addressed during Borderland Foundation's international summer programme The Village of Bridge Builders (13–23 August 2015, Krasnogruda, Poland). It featured participatory artistic and reflective workshops, lectures, and debates related to dialogue and bridge-building in bordering regions all over the world.
The play *The Mystery of the Bridge* concluded the artistic part of the programme.

Borderland, Foundation, *The Mystery of the Bridge* as part of The Village of Bridge Builders event, Krasnogruda 2015. Courtesy: Borderland Foundation. Photo by: Cezary Nowak

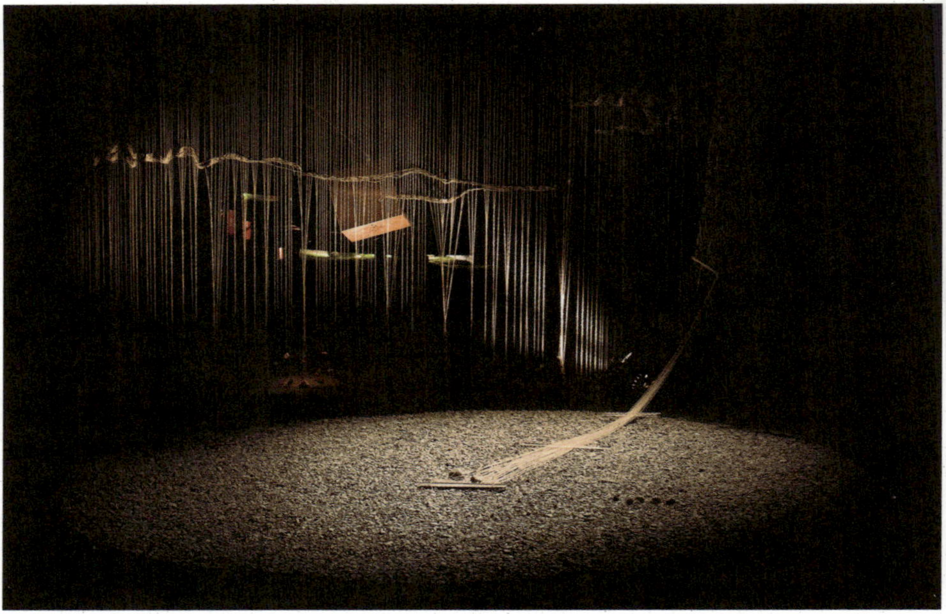

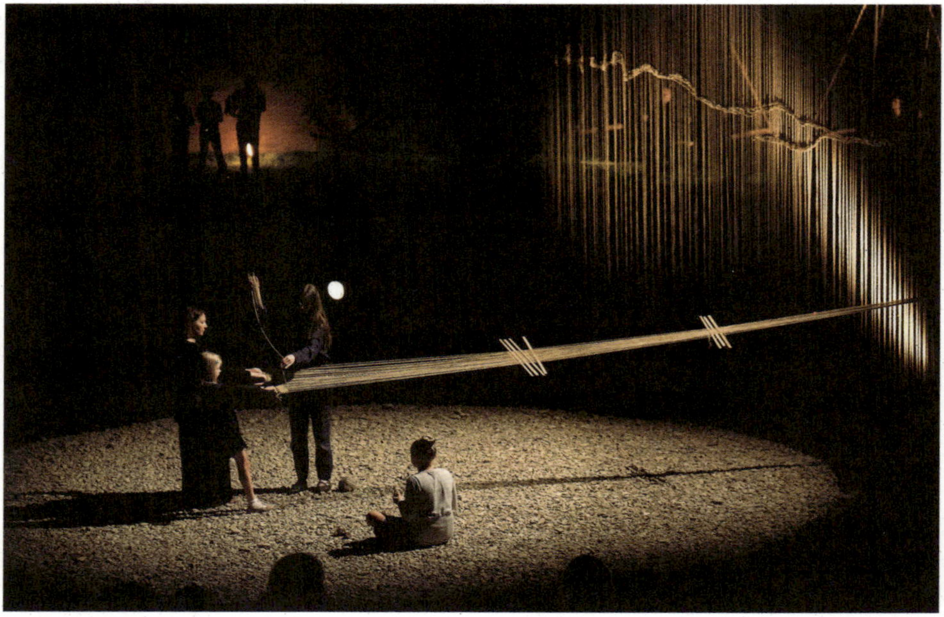

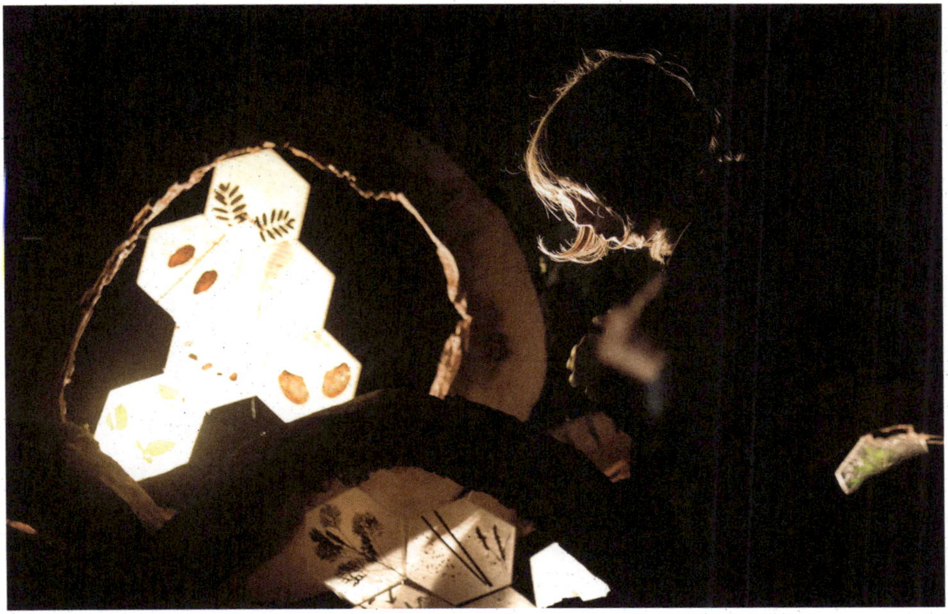

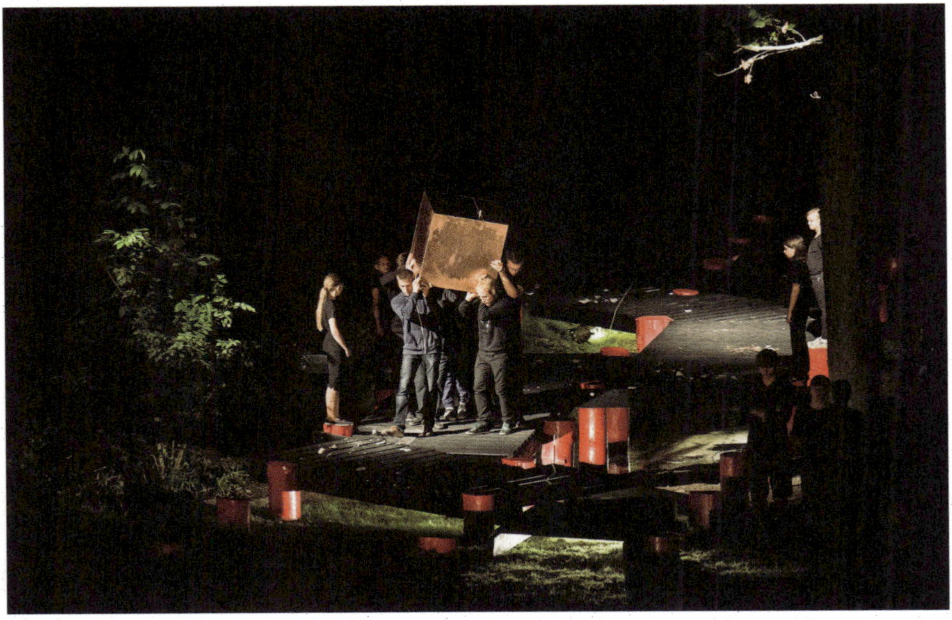

Stefan Kaegi

COURAGEOUS CITIZENS

The unfinished new Berlin airport, the never-ending A3 freeway project in Italy, the soccer arenas in Qatar: delayed completions and cost adjustments, the complex interdependencies of private and public stakeholders, the invisible links throughout the world.... What do mega-construction sites tell us about our society? Why do states build, and for whom? By participation or master plan? In the second part of their tetralogy about post-democratic phenomena, Stefan Kaegi/Rimini Protokoll look at large construction sites as models for the current constitution of society. *Society under Construction/Gesellschaftsmodell Großbaustelle (State 2)* is a production of Rimini Protokoll and the Düsseldorfer Schauspielhaus as part of 100 Years of Now.

Stefan Kaegi/Rimini Protokoll, *Society Under Construction/Gesellschaftsmodell Großbaustelle (State 2)*, 2016, Theatre, stage views. Courtesy: Benno Tobler. Photos by: Benno Tobler

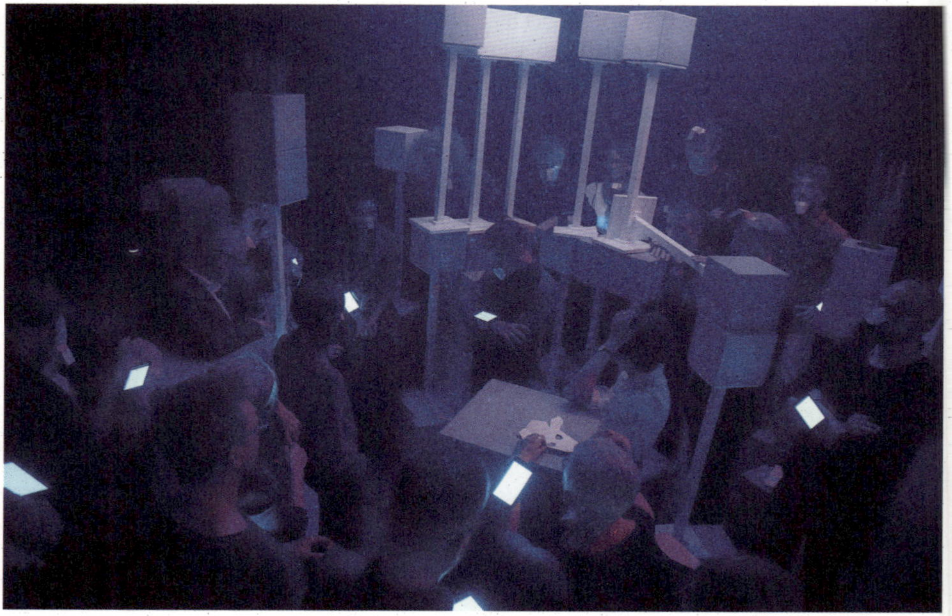

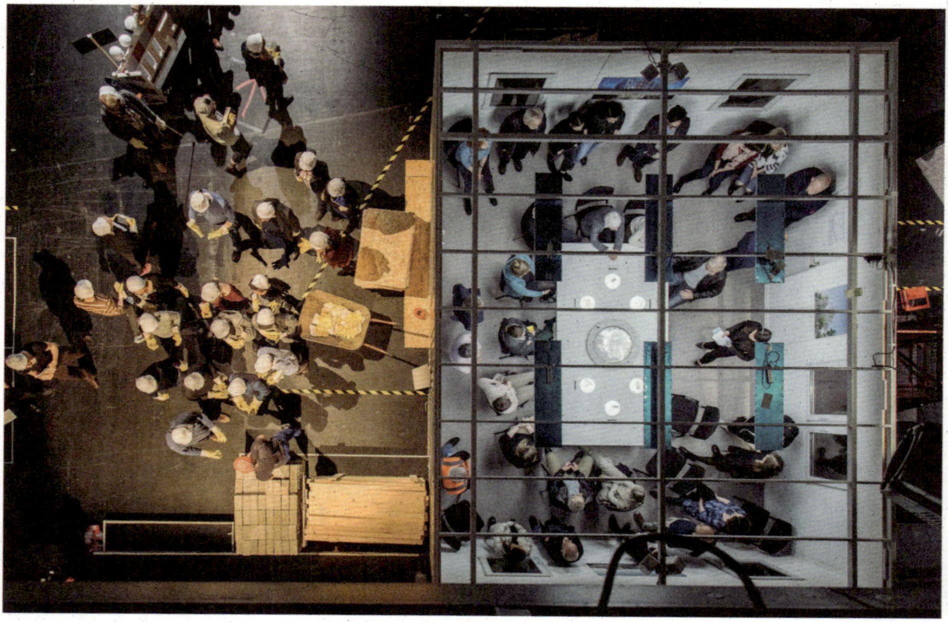

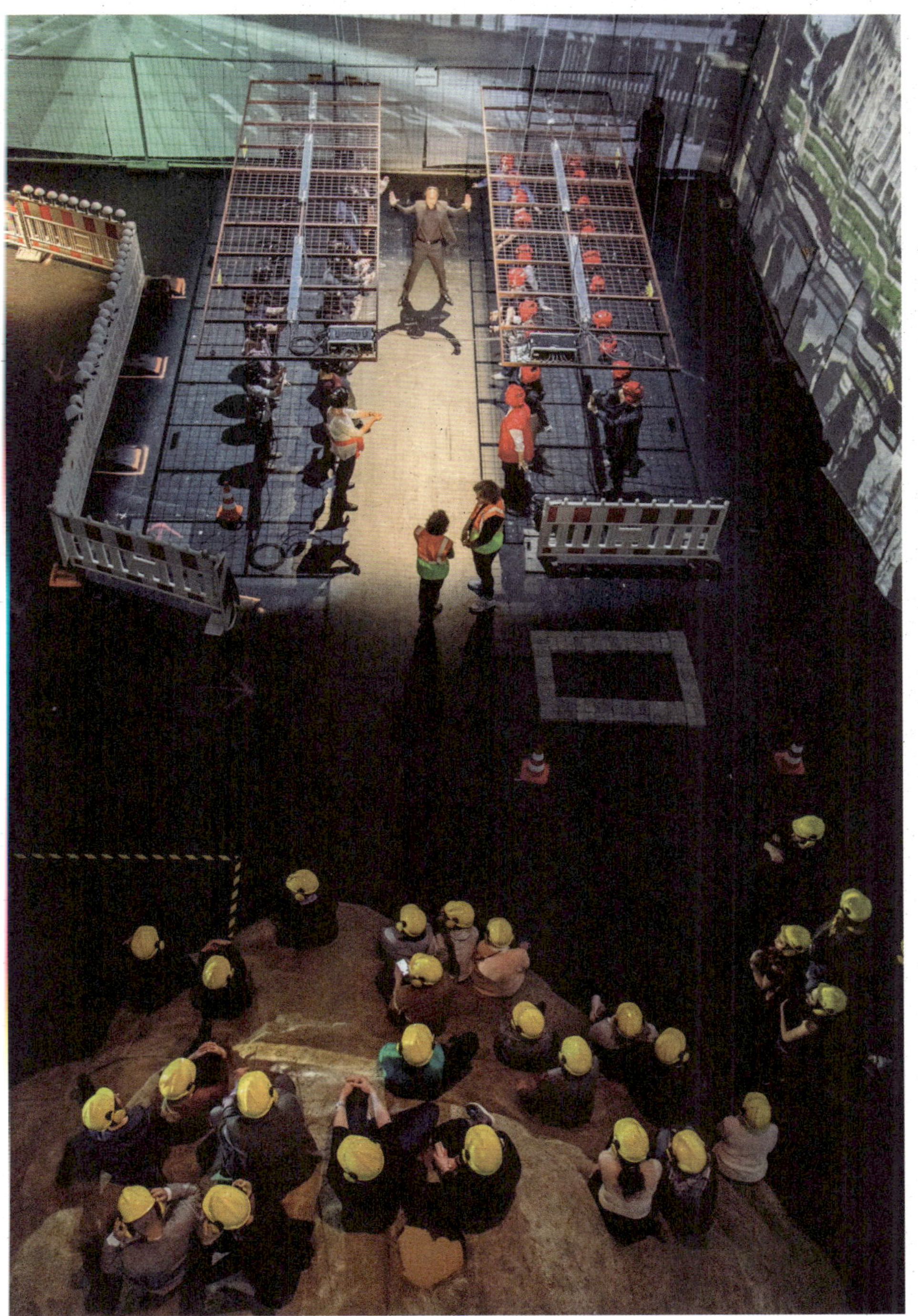

COURAGEOUS CITIZENS

CONTRIBUTORS

JOHN AKOMFRAH is an artist, filmmaker, and cultural activist. His works are characterized by their investigations into memory, post-colonialism, temporality, and aesthetics, and often explore the experiences of migrant diasporas globally. Akomfrah was a founding member of the Black Audio Film Collective, which started in London in 1982. Since 1998, he has been Director of the film and television production company Smoking Dogs Films. His more recent work includes *The Unfinished Conversation* (2012), a portrait of the cultural theorist Stuart Hall's life and work; *Peripeteia* (2012), an imagined drama visualizing the lives of individuals included in two sixteenth-century portraits of Albrecht Dürer; *Mnemosyne* (2010) which exposes the experience of migrants in the UK; and *Vertigo Sea* (2015), which focuses on the disorder and cruelty of the whaling industry and juxtaposes it with scenes of many genera-tions of migrants making epic crossings of the ocean for a better life. Recently, Akomfrah premiered his six-channel video installation *Purple* (2017), which addresses climate change and its effects on human communities, biodiversity, and the wilderness. In 2012, John Akomfrah received the ECF Princess Margaret Award for Culture. www.smokingdogsfilms.com

BORDERLAND FOUNDATION is an educational and cultural organi-zation, a documentation centre, and a publishing house based in Sejny, Poland. Established in 1990 by a group of artists and cultural animators, Borderland's various activities include a teenage theatre group and a klezmer band that perform regularly across the region and internationally; oral history projects that bring together Poles, Lithuanians, Belarusians, Roma, and Russians; meetings and conferences for scholars and cultural practitioners from Poland and beyond; workshops, performances, exhibitions, conferences, cultural forums, and festivals that draw thousands of international visitors and local participants. Borderland's self-defined mission is the reinvention of the agora—a democratic space for the open exchange of ideas in the contemporary world. Their goal is to overcome regional and nationalist divisions and build bridges between local ethnic groups, thus promoting dialogue among various, and at times conflicting, identities, memories, and religions. In 2018, the Borderland Foundation received the ECF Princess Margriet for Culture. www.pogranicze.sejny.pl

ROSI BRAIDOTTI is a Philosopher and Distinguished Professor and founding Director of the Centre for the Humanities at Utrecht University. She was the founding Professor of Gender Studies in the Humanities at Utrecht University (1988–2005) and the first scientific director of the Netherlands Research School of Women's Studies. In 2005–2006, she was the Leverhulme Trust Visiting Professorship in the Law School of Birkbeck College, University of London. In 2001–2003, Braidotti held the Jean Monnet Visiting Chair at the Robert Schuman Centre for Advanced Studies of the European Institute in Florence. In 1994–1995, she was a Fellow in the School of Social Science at the Institute for Advanced Study at Princeton. She has been a visiting professor at the London School of Economics, Birkbeck College, the University of the Arts in London, and the Universities of Bologna, Tampere, Frankfurt, Buenos Aires, and Melbourne, and the European University Institute. www.rosibraidotti.com

VASYL CHEREPANYN is the Director of the Visual Culture Research Center (VCRC) in Kyiv, and an editor of the Ukrainian edition of *Political Critique* magazine. He works as a senior lecturer at the Cultural Studies Department of the National University of Kyiv-Mohyla Academy and holds a PhD in Philosophy. Cherepanyn has also worked as a guest lecturer at the Institute for Advanced Studies of the Political Critique in Warsaw, Poland and the Alfried Krupp Wissenschaftskolleg Greifswald of the Greifswald University, Germany. VCRC was founded in 2008 as a platform for collaboration between academic, artistic, and activist communities. The centre is an independent initiative, engaged in publishing and artistic activities, scientific research, organization of public lectures, discussions, and conferences. In 2015, VCRC received the ECF Princess Margaret Award for Culture. www.vcrc.org.ua

BOJANA CVEJIĆ is a performance theorist and performance maker based in Brussels. She is a co-founding member of TkH editorial collective. Cvejić received her PhD in Philosophy from the Centre for Research in Modern European Philosophy, London, and MA and BA degrees in musicology and aesthetics from the Faculty of Music, University of the Arts, Belgrade. Her latest books are *Choreographing Problems: Expressive Concepts in European Contemporary Dance and Performance* (2016); *Drumming & Rain: A Choreographer's Score*, co-written with A.T. De Keersmaeker (2014); *Parallel Slalom: Lexicon of Nonaligned Poetics*, co-edited with G.S. Pristač (2013); and *Public Sphere by Performance*, co-written with Ana Vujanović (2012). She has been (co-)author, dramaturge or performer in many dance and theatre performances since 1996, and has directed five experimental opera stagings, most notably *Don Giovanni* at BITEF, Belgrade (2008). Cvejić teaches at various dance and performance programmes in Europe and has recently been appointed Professor of Philosophy of Art for the doctoral studies at the Faculty for Media and Communication, University Singidunum in Belgrade. Her current research focuses on social choreography, technologies and performances of the self, and time and rhythm in performance poetics and Post-Fordist modes of production. www.bojanacvejic.info

FATIMA EL-TAYEB is Professor of African-American Literature and Culture and Director of Critical Gender Studies at the University of California, San Diego. She is the author of two books, *European Others: Queering Ethnicity in Postnational Europe* (2011) and *Schwarze Deutsche: Rasse und nationale Identität* (2001), as well as numerous articles on the interactions of race, gender, sexuality, and nation. Before moving to the US, El-Tayeb lived in Germany and the Netherlands, where she was active in black feminist, migrant, and queer of colour organizations. She is co-author of the movie *Alles wird gut/Everything will be fine* (1997).

FORENSIC ARCHITECTURE is an interdisciplinary 'forensic' research agency housed in Goldsmiths University, London, since 2011. Since its founding, Forensic Architecture has been using innovative research methods to undertake a series of investigations into human rights abuses. Forensic Architecture, which was initiated by architect Eyal Weizman, is a multi-disciplinary agency comprised of international artists, media developers, and scientists and has previously investigated war crimes in Gaza, former Yugoslavia, and Syria. They employ architectural know-how, imaging technologies, and aesthetic strategies in order to create a forum, a space of public debate, around the issues that they probe to reveal humanitarian injustice not only in active conflict zones but also in contentious situations within Western European states. Their evidence is presented in arts and cultural, political and legal contexts, including international courts, truth commissions, and human rights and environmental fora. www.forensic-architecture.org

PASCAL GIELEN is Full Professor of Sociology of Art and Politics at the Antwerp Research Institute for the Arts (Antwerp University, Belgium), where he leads the Culture Commons Quest Office (CCQO). Gielen is Editor-in-Chief of the international book series *Arts in Society*. In 2016, he became laureate of the Odysseus grant for excellent international scientific research of the Fund for Scientific Research Flanders in Belgium. His research focuses on creative labour, the institutional context of the arts and cultural politics. Gielen has published many books, which have been translated in English, Korean, Polish, Portuguese, Russian, Spanish, and Turkish. www.ccqo.eu

STUART HALL was a Jamaican-British academic, writer and cultural studies pioneer, who was born in Kingston, Jamaica in 1932 and died in London aged 82 in February 2014. Hall was a Rhodes scholar at Merton College, Oxford, Director of the Birmingham Centre for Contemporary Cultural Studies and Profes-sor of Sociology at the Open University. He was the President of the British Sociological Association and a member of the Runnymede Commission on the Future of Multi-Ethnic Britain. He also chaired the arts organizations Iniva and Autograph ABP. Hall was the first editor of *New Left Review*, a founding editor of the journal *Soundings* and author of many articles and books on politics and culture including *Policing the Crisis* and 'The Great Moving Right Show' (for *Marxism Today*), in which he famously coined the term 'Thatcherism'. A memoir by Stuart Hall, *Familiar Stranger: A Life between Two Islands*, and a collection of his political essays *Selected Political Writings: The Great Moving Right Show* and other essays were published in 2017. In 2008, Stuart Hall received the ECF Princess Margaret Award for Culture. www.stuarthallfoundation.org

DAVID HARVEY is the Distinguished Professor of Anthropology at the Graduate Center of the City University of New York (CUNY) and the Director of Research at the Center for Place, Culture and Politics. He is the author of numerous books, including *Rebel Cities: From the Right to the City to the Urban Revolution* (2012), *The Ways of the World* (2016), and most recently *Marx, Capital and the Madness of Economic Reason* (2017). www.davidharvey.org

STEFAN KAEGI produces documentary theatre plays, radio shows, and works in the urban environment in a variety of collaborative partnerships. Using research, public auditions and conceptual processes, he gives voice to 'experts' who are not trained actors but have something to tell. Kaegi co-produces works with Helgard Haug and Daniel Wetzel, under the label 'Rimini Protokoll'. Rimini Protokoll's purpose is to pry apart the sense of reality and present all its facets from unusual perspectives. www.rimini-protokoll.de/website/en/about-sk

IVAN KRASTEV is the Chairman of the Centre for Liberal Strategies in Sofia and permanent fellow at the Institute for Human Sciences, Vienna. He is a founding board member of the Board of Trustees of the International Crisis Group and is a contributing opinion writer for the *International New York Times*. His latest books in English are *After Europe* (2017); *Democracy Disrupted: The Global Politics on Protest* (2014); *In Mistrust We Trust: Can Democracy Survive When We Don't Trust Our Leaders?* (2013). He is co-author, with Stephen Holmes, of a forthcoming book on Russian politics.

BAS LAFLEUR is a researcher, editor, and bookbinder. In 2010, he received his PhD in Art History at Leiden University. He is co-founder and editor of *Eastern Christian Art in Its Late Antique and Islamic Contexts* (ECA). Bas is the author of *Identity and Christian-Muslim Interaction: Medieval Art of the Syrian Orthodox from the Mosul Area* (2010) and co-editor, together with Odile Chenal, of *Remappings: The Making of European Narratives* (2012). Before starting as a freelance editor and researcher for the European Cultural Foundation, he was a Research Fellow at the Laboratoire d'excellence Religions et Sociétés dans le Monde Méditerranéen (LABEX RESMED) at the Sorbonne in Paris and a Fellow at the Centre of Aramaic Studies at the University of Konstanz.

WIETSKE MAAS is an artist and curator. Based in Amsterdam and Berlin, Wietske combines artistic pursuits with her work as a curatorial advisor for the European Cultural Foundation and as curator of the Research and Fellowship Program at BAK, basis voor actuele kunst, Utrecht.

SUSANNE MORS is publications adviser and editor at the European Cultural Foundation, Amsterdam. Next to that she works as independent supervisor and consultant. Previous fields of work comprise international project management, reflection processes, grant-giving, corporate communications and HRM. She holds a Master's degree in Literature and Cultural Studies from Humboldt University Berlin and is also trained in the field of organization development at Utrecht University. www.culturalfoundation.eu

MARINA NAPRUSHKINA is a Berlin-based artist and activist. Since 2007, she has organized multi-media projects under the imaginary Office for Anti-Propaganda, including videos, installations, and newspapers. Informed by her own experience growing up in Belarus, Naprushkina examines the structure of authoritarian systems to determine the role of art and creative activism in changing the political status quo. In 2013, she founded Neue Nachbarschaft//Moabit, a self-organizing community in Moabit, where a growing community of more than 500 old and new Berliners are finding collaborative ways of living together. Naprushkina is the author of *Neue Heimat? Wie Flüchtlinge uns zu besseren Nachbarn Machen* (2015). In 2017, she received the ECF Princess Margriet Award for Culture. www.neuenachbarschaft.de

LIA PERJOVSCHI is an artist, curator, and cultural activist currently based in Bucharest, where she studied at the Art Academy. She has been recognized as one of the leading performance artists in Romania, and is also known for her unusual objects. After the fall of communism, she has tried to bring information to Romania that citizens had no access to under their tightly controlled state. Since 1989, she has gradually focused on more conceptual projects such as the creation of archives, diagrams, and information rooms that tell various modern histories and visually demonstrate how we organize history. Lia Perjovschi is the founder and coordinator of the Contemporary Art Archive and Center for Art Analysis (CAA/CAA) and the Knowledge Museum in Sibiu, Romania. Amongst her recent solo exhibitions are *Lia Perjovschi Knowledge Museum* (MUSAC, León; 2015); *Dan Perjovschi: Time Specific, Lia Perjovschi: Knowledge Museum Kit* (Rupert Centre for Art and Education, Vilnius; 2014); *Lieber Aby Warburg, was tun mit den Bildern? Vom Umgang mit fotografischem Material* (Museum für Gegenwartskunst, Siegen; 2012); and *JUST ANOTHER BRICK IN THE WALL: MODELS OF ART PRODUCTION IN ROMANIA* (Barbara Seiler Gallery, Zürich;

2011). In 2013, Lia and her husband, the artist Dan Perjovschi, received the ECF Princess Margriet Award for Culture.

SASKIA SASSEN is the Robert S. Lynd Professor of Sociology at Columbia University and a Member of its Committee on Global Thought, which she chaired until 2015. She is a student of cities, immigration, and states in the world economy, with inequality, gendering, and digitalization as three key variables running through her work. Born in the Netherlands, she grew up in Argentina and Italy, studied in France, was raised in five languages, and began her professional life in the United States. She is the author of eight books and the editor or co-editor of three more. Together, her authored books are translated in over twenty languages. Sassen received many awards and honours, among them multiple doctor honoris causa, the 2013 Principe de Asturias Prize in the Social Sciences, election to the Royal Academy of the Sciences of the Netherlands, and made a Chevalier de l'Ordre des Arts et Lettres by the French government. Her most recent book is *Expulsions: Brutality and Complexity in the Global Economy* (2014). www.saskiasassen.com

ANA VUJANOVIĆ is a cultural worker—and a researcher, writer, dramaturge, and activist—in the fields of contemporary performing arts and culture. In 2004, she received her PhD in Theatre Studies at the Faculty of Dramatic Arts, University of Arts in Belgrade. She was a member of the editorial collective TkH, a Belgrade-based theoretical-artistic platform, and Editor-in-Chief of the *TkH Journal for Performing Arts Theory* (2000–2017). A particular commitment of hers has been to empower independent scenes in Belgrade and throughout former Yugoslavia. She has lectured at various universities and educational programmes throughout Europe, was a visiting professor at the Performance Studies Department of the University of Hamburg, and since 2016 she is a team member and mentor of fourth-year students at SDNO—School for New Dance Development in Amsterdam. Vujanović participates in art projects in the fields of performance, theatre, dance, and video/film, as a dramaturge and co-author. She has published a number of articles in journals and collections and authored four books, most recently *Public Sphere by Performance*, with Bojana Cvejić (2012). Currently she is working on a research project, *Performing the Self in the 21st Century*, again together with Bojana Cvejić. www.anavujanovic.net

KATHERINE WATSON moved from Canada to join the European Cultural Foundation in 2006 and has been Director since 2010. Prior to working with ECF, Katherine's international experience, from both sides of the Atlantic, has combined interdisciplinary production with advocacy, research, policy and programme development for non-profit arts and culture organizations and all levels of government. She has a particular interest in investigating the impact of the digital shift on our lives, in fostering the intersection of art and culture with other fields of endeavour, and in enabling voices from all corners of civil society. Katherine is the Cultural Leader in Residence for a Research Masters Programme in Cultural Leadership at Groningen University. She is currently Vice Chair of the European Foundation Centre, a membership organization for institutional philanthropy that was instigated by ECF and in which ECF plays an active part. www.culturalfoundation.eu

10 YEARS ECF PRINCESS MARGRIET AWARD FOR CULTURE—
ACKNOWLEDGEMENTS

Since its establishment in 2008, the ECF Princess Margriet Award
for Culture is a platform for acknowledging those whose creative
work can truly make a difference to Europe's varied societies.
The Award underlines the European Cultural Foundation's belief
that social and political change requires artistic and cultural
engagement. It was initiated in honour of the organization's former
President, HRH Princess Margriet of the Netherlands, who has
shown enormous dedication to the important role of culture
in invigorating democracy in Europe. The Award was established
in partnership with (and between 2008–2011 supported by) the
Dutch Ministry of Education, Culture, and Science and the Dutch
Ministry of Foreign Affairs.
www.culturalfoundation.eu/pma

Laureates 2008–2018

2008 · Jérôme Bel & Pichet Klunchun
· Stuart Hall

2010 · Stefan Kaegi
· Borka Pavićević

2011 · Kutluğ Ataman
· Šejla Kamerić

2012 · John Akomfrah
· Charles Esche

2013 · Yoel Gamzou
· Lia & Dan Perjovschi

2014 · Teodor Celakoski
· Teatro Valle Occupato

2015 · Athens Biennale
· Visual Culture Research Center

2016 · Krétakör
· Medialab-Prado

2017 · Aslı Erdoğan
· Navid Kermani
· Luc Mishalle
· Marina Naprushkina

2018 · Borderland Foundation
· Forensic Architecture

Jury

Laureates are selected by an international, interdisciplinary, and independent Jury, convening each year in person to assess the shortlisted nominations. Jury members are listed below with the affiliation they held during their Jury membership.

- Rachida Azough (2008–2010), Creative Director, Kosmopolis, Rotterdam
- Tessa Boerman (2017–today), Filmmaker, Amsterdam
- Iara Boubnova (2008–2011), Founding Director, Institute of Contemporary Art, Sofia
- Andreas Broeckmann (2015–today), Curator, Leuphana Arts Program, Lüneburg/Berlin
- Hilary Carty (2010–2012), Director, Cultural Leadership Programme, London
- Bojana Cvejić (2014–2016), Performance theorist and maker, Brussels/Belgrade
- Sudeep Dasgupta (2010–2012), Associate Professor, Department of Media & Culture, University of Amsterdam
- Chris Dercon (2014–2016), Director, Tate Modern, London
- Jan Dibbets (2012–2013), Artist, Amsterdam
- Christian Esch (2013–2014), Director, NRW Kultursekretariat, Wuppertal
- Juan Freire (2015–today), Academic Dean, Tecnológico de Monterrey Business School, Mexico City
- Ivan Krastev (2016–today), Chairman of the Centre for Liberal Strategies, Vienna
- Maria Lind (2011–2013), Director, Tensta Konsthall, Stockholm
- Ruth Mackenzie (2016–today), Artistic Director, Holland Festival, Amsterdam and Artistic Director, Châtelet Theatre, Paris
- Robert Palmer (2008–2011), Director of Culture, Cultural and Natural Heritage, Council of Europe, Strasbourg
- Mike Phillips (2008–2010), historian, novelist, and curator, London
- Els van der Plas (2012–2014), General Director, Muziektheater, Amsterdam
- Saskia van Stein (2015–2017), Director, Bureau Europa, platform for architecture & design, Maastricht
- Rana Zincir Celal (2013–2014), Program Manager, Columbia Global Centers | Turkey and Executive Board Member, Anadolu Kültür, Istanbul

COURAGEOUS CITIZENS

Nominators

Each edition, the European Cultural Foundation invites a different set of cultural professionals from various disciplines with broad perspectives on cultural and artistic practice to submit their confidential nominations. Since the beginning of the Award we have worked with approximately 330 nominators. They come from more than 36 countries in wider Europe, and include independent experts brought forward through ECF's broader network, as well as individuals and organizations who through various programmes and grant schemes were part of ECF's community of practice in past years. This resulted in more than 400 nominations throughout the past 10 years. We thank all nominators for their invaluable contribution to the Award.

COURAGEOUS CITIZENS

The design and form of this book take their cue from the many ideas proposed
by the writers in the book, and emphasizes diversity, exchange, and movement.
Instead of imposing a single tone and homogeneous environment on the texts,
perspectives are shifted and relocation and unexpected combinations of voices
are proposed. There are no marginalized characters, as each voice has the
opportunity to carry the main text or support the navigation through the book.
As the environment and conditions are constantly changing, they call for
a new language of diversity and adaptation.

COURAGEOUS CITIZENS
How Culture Contributes
to Social Change

Editors
BAS LAFLEUR, WIETSKE MAAS
and SUSANNE MORS

Managing editor
SUSANNE MORS

Editorial Advice
ENRICA FLORES D'ARCAIS
PIA POL

Contributors
ROSI BRAIDOTTI
VASYL CHEREPANYN
BOJANA CVEJIĆ
FATIMA EL-TAYEB
PASCAL GIELEN
STUART HALL
DAVID HARVEY
IVAN KRASTEV
WIETSKE MAAS
MARINA NAPRUSHKINA
SASKIA SASSEN
ANA VUJANOVIĆ
KATHERINE WATSON

Artistic Contributions
JOHN AKOMFRAH
BORDERLAND FOUNDATION
FORENSIC ARCHITECTURE
STEFAN KAEGI
LIA PERJOVSCHI

Translation
ALICE TETLEY-PAUL
(text MARINA NAPRUSHKINA,
German-English)

Copy Editing
LEO REIJNEN

Proofreading
ELS BRINKMAN

Design
ELISABETH KLEMENT
and JAN TOMSON

Typefaces
Hiragino Kaku Gothic, Stanley
Smith, Times New Roman,
Tzaristane Cal, Vomit Police,
Vonnes

Paper Inside
Oikos Extra white, Splendorgel
Extra White, Symbol Freelife
Gloss Premium White

Paper Cover
Oikos Extra white

Printing and Binding
Bariet/Ten Brink, Meppel

Publisher
PIA POL,
ASTRID VORSTERMANS /
VALIZ, AMSTERDAM

Courageous Citizens is published on
the occasion of the 10th anniversary
of the ECF Princess Margriet Award
for Culture (PMA), an annual award
acknowledging the work of individuals
and collectives whose creative work
can truly make a difference in Europe's
societies.

COURAGEOUS CITIZENS

This publication was published in partnership with:

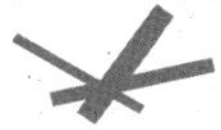

European Cultural Foundation

The European Cultural Foundation is an independent, impact driven organization with almost sixty-five years of experience. It catalyses, connects and communicates civil society initiatives in arts and culture to work together for an open, democratic and inclusive Europe. The European Cultural Foundation supports cultural changemakers through grants, exchanges, and incubator programmes. Its annual ECF Princess Margriet Award for Culture highlights culture as a force for positive change. The foundation connects people to people, the local to the European, and grassroots to policy.
www.culturalfoundation.eu

Valiz is an independent international publisher on contemporary art, design, theory, critique, typography and urban affairs, based in Amsterdam. Our books offer critical reflection, interdisciplinary inspiration, and establish a connection between cultural disciplines and socio-economic, political questions. Our programme consists of two components:
· theory and texts on art and visual culture;
· books that are conceived and elaborated in close collaboration with artists, designers and art institutes.
Apart from publishing Valiz organizes cultural projects in which certain topics in contemporary art, politics and culture are investigated.
www.valiz.nl

DISTRIBUTION
BE/NL/LU: Centraal Boekhuis,
   www.cb.nl
GB/IE: Anagram Books,
   www.anagrambooks.com
Europe/Asia: Idea Books,
   www.ideabooks.nl
Australia: Perimeter Books,
   www.perimeterdistribution.com
USA: D.A.P., www.artbook.com
Individual orders: www.valiz.nl;
info@valiz.nl

ISBN 978 94 92095 51 0
Printed and bound in the EU
Valiz, Amsterdam, 2018

COURAGEOUS CITIZENS